EVIDENCE BASED PRIMARY TEACHING

JONATHAN GLAZZARD AND SAMUEL STONES

EVIDENCE BASED PRIMARY TEACHING

LM Learning Matters

Learning Matters
A SAGE Publishing Company
1 Oliver's Yard
55 City Road
London EC1Y 1SP

SAGE Publications Inc.
2455 Teller Road
Thousand Oaks, California 91320

SAGE Publications India Pvt Ltd
B 1/I 1 Mohan Cooperative Industrial Area
Mathura Road
New Delhi 110 044

SAGE Publications Asia-Pacific Pte Ltd
3 Church Street
#10-04 Samsung Hub
Singapore 049483

Editor: Amy Thornton
Senior project editor: Chris Marke
Project management: River Editorial & Publishing
Services
Marketing manager: Lorna Patkai
Cover design: Wendy Scott
Typeset by: C&M Digitals (P) Ltd, Chennai, India
Printed in the UK

First published in 2021

Library of Congress Control Number: 2020942868

British Library Cataloguing in Publication Data

A catalogue record for this book is available from
the British Library

ISBN 978-1-5297-4193-3
ISBN 978-1-5297-4192-6 (pbk)

At SAGE we take sustainability seriously. Most of our products are printed in the UK using responsibly sourced
papers and boards. When we print overseas we ensure sustainable papers are used as measured by the
PREPS grading system. We undertake an annual audit to monitor our sustainability.

CONTENTS

About the authors   vii
Introduction   ix

1   Early years pedagogy   1

2   How children learn   10

3   Memory   25

4   Subject knowledge   36

5   Modelling   46

6   Inclusion   56

7   Assessment for learning   74

8   Behaviour   85

9   Metacognition   96

Conclusion   105
References   107
Index   120

ABOUT THE AUTHORS

Jonathan Glazzard is Professor of Teacher Education and Head of Department for Children, Education and Communities at Edge Hill University. He is an active researcher and teacher educator as well as a qualified teacher. Jonathan taught in state primary schools for 10 years before moving into higher education. His research addresses issues of inclusion and social justice within education.

Samuel Stones is Associate Researcher in the Carnegie School of Education at Leeds Beckett University. His research outputs are linked with the Centre for LGBTQ+ Inclusion in Education and the Carnegie Centre of Excellence for Mental Health in Schools. Samuel's research explores the experiences of teachers who identify as lesbian, gay, bisexual and transgender, with specific emphasis on the impact of sexual orientation on teacher identity and mental health. He also works with initial teacher training students in university and school contexts and is an associate leader of maths, computing, economics and business at a secondary school and sixth form college in North Yorkshire.

INTRODUCTION

This book focuses on the evidence that underpins effective primary teaching. It presents research and theories which underpin specific approaches that primary school teachers use in their teaching.

In recent years, there has been a move towards more evidence-informed teaching in schools worldwide. This is demonstrated by the development of a range of organisations, including the Education Endowment Foundation (EEF), the Chartered College of Teaching, the National Foundation for Educational Research (NFER) and the Institute for Effective Education (IEE).

The *Carter Review* highlighted that 'new teachers need to be taught how to become intelligent consumers of research' (Carter, 2015, p28). In effect, this means being able to search for and access a range of research studies, the skill of synthesising large amounts of information, and the ability to critically analyse research findings. Theory, research and practice should be seamlessly linked. Without an understanding of research and theory, there is no robust rationale for using specific approaches in the classroom. Understanding the research that underpins specific approaches enables trainee teachers and teachers to articulate a rationale for their practice and to defend the pedagogical approaches that they employ in the classroom.

That said, teachers are extremely busy. Teacher education courses are demanding and time-limited. Teaching is a busy profession. Teachers may want to read in-depth studies but often they do not have the time or energy to do so, particularly after a busy day in the classroom. This book synthesises some of the key research findings and presents them concisely so that trainees and teachers can access the key findings quickly and efficiently.

It is sad that some trainees and teachers hold the view that research and theory are irrelevant. Some disengage from research, and there are those who just want 'quick fixes' or solutions to classroom problems or others who just want 'top tips' for teaching. We argue that this is a narrow view and restricts teacher professional development. There are also others who feel that teachers do not have the intellectual capacity to engage with research and theory and hold the assumption that teachers lack interest in theoretical underpinning. We believe that this is an incorrect assumption to make and extremely offensive. We have worked with and alongside many teachers who value research and theory, who are interested in both, and who use research and theory to improve their own practice. Many teachers have an appetite for research. They want to know the latest research findings and are interested in how they can use these findings to improve their own practice.

UNDERSTANDING THE **RESEARCH** THAT UNDERPINS SPECIFIC APPROACHES **ENABLES** TRAINEE TEACHERS AND TEACHERS TO **ARTICULATE** A RATIONALE FOR THEIR **PRACTICE** AND TO **DEFEND** THE **PEDAGOGICAL APPROACHES** THAT THEY EMPLOY IN THE CLASSROOM.

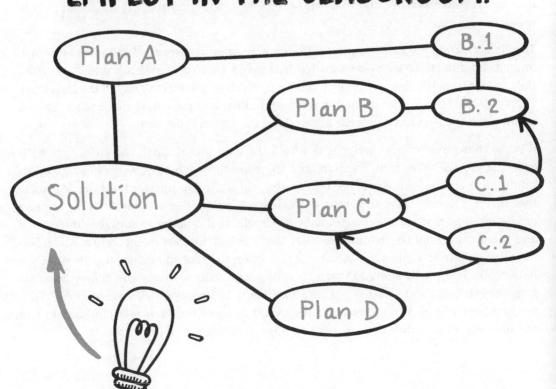

This book is structured broadly, but not completely, in line with the teachers' standards. Each chapter positions the content within a broader policy context. Key research is stated in each chapter and each chapter includes examples of best practice.

1
EARLY YEARS PEDAGOGY

IN THIS CHAPTER

This chapter introduces you to the key research on effective pedagogy in the early years. It emphasises the importance of play-based learning, practitioner intervention in children's play and the importance of balancing child-initiated play with adult-directed learning. It argues that the 'schoolification' of early years practice is potentially damaging because children may miss out on aspects of learning that are critical to securing long-term academic outcomes. Effective practice is illustrated through case studies.

KEY RESEARCH

Seminal research in the early years concludes:

- Child-initiated play, combined with the provision of teacher-initiated group work, is the most effective vehicle for learning.

- Practitioner intervention in children's freely chosen play is an effective strategy for providing intellectual challenge. Weisberg et al. (2013) refer to this strategy as 'guided play'. Guided play is neither direct teaching nor free play, but it sits between these two pedagogical approaches.

- The most effective pedagogy combines both 'teaching' and the provision of freely chosen yet potentially instructive play activities.

- The use of 'sustained shared thinking' was observed in settings where children made the most progress.

- The modelling skills or appropriate behaviour by adults were often combined with sustained periods of shared thinking in effective settings.

- Open-ended questioning and modelling were also associated with better cognitive achievement.

- Effective pedagogy for young children is less formal than for primary school.

- The most effective settings adopted discipline/behaviour policies in which staff supported children in rationalising and talking through their conflicts.

(Sylva et al., 2004)

Goswami and Bryant (2007) report evidence from neuroscience which has shown that learning depends on neural networking across visual, auditory and kinaesthetic brain regions. These findings indicate that opportunities for multisensory, active learning are critical to promoting academic and social outcomes for children in the early years.

Research also demonstrates that children who enter school with poorly developed speech and language are at high risk of literacy difficulties (Snowling et al., 2011). The focus on supporting children's communication and language development is therefore crucial in the early years, particularly for children who enter early years settings with underdeveloped skills in this domain.

The importance of developing children's social and emotional regulation skills and promoting a positive sense of self in the early years has been identified by researchers. Developing these aspects supports positive longer-term outcomes (Goodman et al., 2015).

Researchers have also identified the importance of developing executive functioning skills in the early years to support long-term attainment. These include:

- *Cognitive flexibility.* The ability to switch perspectives.

- *Inhibitory control.* The ability to stay focused despite distraction, to have selective focused attention, and to stay on task.

- *Working memory.* The ability to hold information in the mind, mentally work with it, make sense of what unfolds over time, link learning, reason, remember multiple instructions in sequence, and follow them step by step in the correct order.

(Diamond, 2013)

The research suggests that a combination of play-based learning combined with teacher-directed learning is essential to support children's development. Limiting exposure to play will restrict opportunities to develop children's social and emotional regulation skills and their executive functioning skills. In addition, restricted opportunities for children to engage in play will limit opportunities for sustained shared thinking and exposure to language and vocabulary.

KEY POLICY

In England, at the policy level, there is an assumption that the reception year at the end of the early years foundation stage should prepare children for the national curriculum, and should therefore become increasingly formal. In England in recent years, there has been an increasing prominence of a school readiness agenda and the accompanying 'schoolification' of early years pedagogy. Policy emphasises a pedagogy that promotes school readiness in the final year of the early years foundation stage. This is associated with a more formal and restricted curriculum that does not align with the principles of effective early years pedagogy. This approach effectively restricts exposure to a broad, rich, play-based curriculum in the early years, which is counterproductive to long-term outcomes.

The controversial Ofsted publication *Bold Beginnings* reflects the promotion of a school readiness agenda towards the end of the early years foundation stage in England. Key recommendations from this report include the following:

- Make sure that the teaching of reading, including systematic synthetic phonics, is the core purpose of the reception year.

- Attach greater importance to the teaching of numbers.

- Ensure that when children are learning to write, resources are suitable for their stage of development and that they are taught correct pencil grip and how to sit correctly at a table.

- Devote sufficient time each day to the direct teaching of reading, writing and mathematics.

(Ofsted, 2017, p7)

The emphasis in this report on the teaching of mathematics and literacy skills may result in a formal curriculum in the early years by limiting children's exposure to play. In addition, it can result in communication and language as well as personal and physical development being marginalised, despite the fact that development in these areas is critical to securing good academic outcomes. It is essential that children in the early years are provided with learning opportunities that are developmentally appropriate. For example, children's writing skills may be impeded because they have underdeveloped motor skills. These children may require a motor skills intervention as a prerequisite to holding a pencil. Exposure to spoken language and vocabulary underpins literacy development. A stimulating, high-quality play-based curriculum will immerse children in language and support subsequent development in literacy. If children's development is rushed, the underpinning foundations may not be in place to secure positive long-term outcomes.

BALANCING PEDAGOGICAL APPROACHES

The research cited above suggests that children in the early years need a variety of pedagogical approaches. These include child-initiated play and adult-initiated interactions that are more typically associated with the word 'teaching'. In effective settings, the balance of who initiates the activities (i.e. children or adults) should be roughly equal (Sylva et al., 2004). Adult intervention in child-initiated play is an effective strategy that provides children with intellectual challenge. Adults can intervene in children's play to model skills, behaviour and language, or they can intervene to promote thinking through the use of high-quality open-ended questioning. Adult intervention in play can support children to operate at a higher level of development but it requires a high degree of practitioner skill. It is less effective when adults intervene and effectively close down children's play. A skilled practitioner can intervene and still allow the child to lead the play rather than imposing their own agenda on the play.

THE IMPORTANCE OF PERSONAL, SOCIAL AND EMOTIONAL DEVELOPMENT

Personal, social and emotional development is the foundation of all learning in the early years. Children cannot learn effectively if they do not establish secure relationships with practitioners in the setting and if they do not feel safe. It is critical to invest time in establishing positive relationships with children through high-quality caring, nurturing interactions.

Children do not necessarily arrive in the setting with good social and emotional regulation skills. A play-based pedagogy in the early years supports the development of these skills because it enables children to interact with others, and to do this effectively they need to learn how to socially interact, how to behave and how to regulate their feelings.

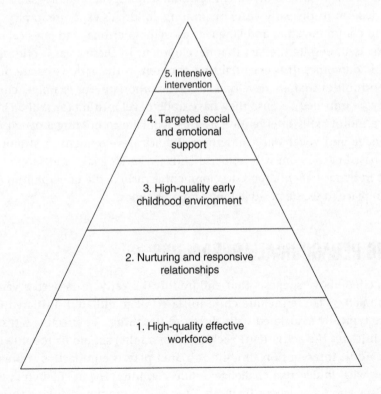

Figure 1.1

Center on the Social and Emotional Foundations for Early Learning (CSEFEL) (http://csefel.vanderbilt.edu/csefelindex.html)

Personal, social and emotional development is the foundation of all learning in the early years.

Children cannot learn effectively if they do not establish secure relationships with practitioners in the setting and if they do not feel safe.

It is CRITICAL to INVEST TIME in establishing positive relationships with children through high-quality, caring, nurturing interactions.

Positive lifetime outcomes are dependent upon a balance of cognitive, social and emotional skills during childhood (OECD, 2015). In addition, research has shown that developing emotional skills along with social skills correlates positively with academic achievement (Durlak et al., 2011; Gutman and Schoon, 2013). Many researchers now agree that emotional development plays a critical role in children's overall well-being and their capacity to form and sustain relationships across the life course (Bowlby, 1988; Denham et al., 2015; Dowling, 2010; Gerhardt, 2014; Thompson and Lagattuta, 2006).

The pyramid model provides a conceptual framework for supporting young children's social and emotional development. We have represented it in Figure 1.1.

The model is based on systematic research that emphasises the importance of the aspects shown on the model to support children's emotional development. The model identifies universal practices that all children need (1, 2, 3). Additionally, some children may need specific targeted social and emotional interventions (4). Finally, a small minority of children may need highly personalised individual social and emotional interventions (5).

EXECUTIVE FUNCTIONING

Executive functioning skills support children to persist with activities and to process multiple instructions at the same time. Practitioners can support the development of these skills by gradually extending the number of instructions they give to children. In addition, instructions can be presented visually so that children have a visual reminder of what they need to do next. Practitioners can intervene in children's play to model the skill of perseverance.

TALKING THROUGH CONFLICT

The research demonstrates that in less effective early years settings, children were simply told to stop inappropriate behaviour (Sylva et al., 2004). In high-quality settings, children are supported by practitioners to talk through conflict. Adults can model this initially by demonstrating the skills of effective listening and communication (e.g. use of turn-taking, eye contact and gesture). Adults can support children during these conversations to encourage them to follow simple rules (e.g. not talking over each other). Eventually, adults can withdraw and allow children to talk through the conflict and find solutions to resolve the situation.

SOCIAL AND EMOTIONAL REGULATION

Roffey (2017) emphasises the importance of social and emotional learning in the early years. Children's social and emotional development will have been influenced by their interactions with significant others and the communities in which they live. The basic premise of social learning theory is that children will replicate the behaviour they have been exposed to (Bandura, 1977). If children have not been provided with clear boundaries in the context of the home, they may come into the early years setting thinking that specific behaviours which are tolerated in the home will also be tolerated in the preschool, nursery or school. They will quickly encounter resistance to negative behaviours, but they need to be given time to accommodate these new expectations. Their behaviours rarely alter overnight. In addition, children's social and emotional behaviours may be an attempt to communicate an unmet need. Children who experience adverse situations in their homes and communities may demonstrate a range of inappropriate behaviours, and practitioners need to be sensitive to the reasons why these behaviours may occur.

TAKE 5

- Play-based pedagogy enhances children's learning in the early years, particularly if adults intervene in instructive play to extend children's learning.

- A balance of adult-led and self-chosen activities provide the optimum conditions for children to learn.

- Settings that focus on the teaching of basic skills in literacy and numeracy alongside play-based learning provide optimum conditions for children's learning.

- Practitioners should support children to talk through conflict.

- Personal, social and emotional development underpins all other aspects of learning in the early years.

CLASSROOM EXAMPLE

An early years setting introduced a social and emotional regulation programme. Children were taught about how to adjust their behaviour in formal and informal situations. They were taught the skills associated with being a good listener and the skills associated with being a good friend. Through stories and puppets, they were introduced to a variety of different feelings. Children were taught how to respond to the feelings of others in a sensitive way. They were also taught about the impact of their words and actions on the feelings of others. In addition, children were taught some practical strategies to support them in managing their feelings. By the end of the intervention, they knew what to do if they felt angry, sad, frightened or frustrated. They were also introduced to both positive and negative feelings.

WHAT DOES GOOD PRACTICE IN SUSTAINED SHARED THINKING LOOK LIKE IN THE CLASSROOM?

Sustained shared thinking is a process that occurs between an adult and a child. It involves skilful higher-order questioning. Within an episode, the adult takes the lead from a child and seizes an opportunity to advance the child's thinking. The research demonstrates that high-quality early years settings are characterised by frequent episodes of sustained shared thinking (Sylva et al., 2004). An example of sustained shared thinking in practice is illustrated through the example below.

The following dialogue between a child and an adult illustrates sustained shared thinking. Notice what the practitioner is doing to advance the child's learning.

A child notices that a puddle is shrinking.

Child: That puddle was massive this morning.

Adult: Why was it so big?

Child: Because it had been raining.

Adult: So why has it got smaller?

Child: Because it has stopped raining.

Adult: Good, because it has stopped raining the puddle won't get any bigger, but why is it drying up and shrinking?

Child: I'm not sure.

Adult: Can you think of anything else that dries up? Maybe something at home?

Child: When the clothes are wet, they dry up.

Adult: Good, where are the clothes?

Child: On the washing line.

Adult: So what makes them go dry?

Child: The sun.

Adult: Brilliant, so why is the puddle drying up?

Child: I think the heat from the sun is drying it up.

Adult: Yes, fantastic! The heat from the sun dries the puddle and it shrinks.

CHAPTER CHECKLIST

	Accessed	Secure	Confident
Know that:			
a combination of pedagogical approaches provides the optimum conditions to support children's learning			
Know how to:			
plan for child-initiated learning			
plan for adult-directed learning			
observe children in the early years and make judgements about their development			
support children's development across all areas of learning			

2
HOW CHILDREN LEARN

IN THIS CHAPTER

This chapter introduces you to key research on children's learning and development. It explains the factors which affect brain development and that the structure of the brain is influenced by the micro and macro contexts within which an individual is situated. Behaviourist, constructivist and social constructivist approaches to learning are outlined, and examples of each provided to support your understanding in relation to these perspectives. It outlines existing research in relation to intelligence and in doing so argues that intelligence is not fixed, and that good teaching can therefore promote brain growth and intelligence.

KEY RESEARCH

The evidence from research has demonstrated:

- Children's learning and development are shaped by a combination of environmental factors and learning opportunities both inside and outside schools.

- Learning involves physical, psychological, social and emotional processes. These influence one another in that the interactions between these processes can enable or restrict learning.

- The brain and intelligence are malleable and can be changed by environmental influences, including exposure to high-quality teaching.

- Our experiences activate neural pathways that enable new ways of thinking and new skills to develop.

- Emotions and social contexts shape neural connections that contribute to attention, concentration and memory, as well as knowledge transfer and application. Research has demonstrated that chronic stress due to trauma affects cognition and working memory.

- Differentiated instruction enables optimum brain growth.

(Darling-Hammond et al., 2019)

KEY POLICY

The teachers' standards state that teachers must:

- demonstrate knowledge and understanding of how pupils learn and how this impacts on teaching.

(DfE, 2011)

WHAT DO WE KNOW ABOUT CHILD DEVELOPMENT?

Bronfenbrenner's (1992) bioecological model has been influential in helping us to understand the internal and external factors that affect child development. The model is represented below (Figure 2.1).

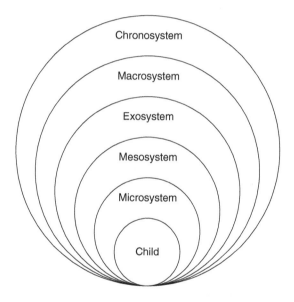

Figure 2.1

- *Child.* The child is surrounded by external influences.

- *Microsystem.* This layer relates to influences that are close to the child, including parents, siblings or the school environment.

- *Mesosystem.* This layer concerns the interactions between people within the microsystem (e.g. the interactions between parents and teachers, and the impact of these interactions on the child).

- *Exosystem.* This layer concerns factors that may not directly impact on the child but may indirectly impact on them (e.g. if a parent becomes unemployed, this can influence the child biologically, socially and psychologically).

- *Macrosystem.* This layer relates to external influences that impact on the child which the child may not even be aware of (e.g. the influences of religion, culture and societal belief on the child's development).

- *Chronosystem.* This layer concerns transitions over the life course that may affect the child's development (e.g. parental separation or changes in national policy and legislation that impact on the child).

WHAT DO WE KNOW ABOUT BRAIN DEVELOPMENT?

Research demonstrates that:

> *Experience is a 'stressor' to brain growth – throughout life, interpersonal experiences and relational connections activate neural pathways, generating energy flow through electrical impulses that strengthen connectivity.*
>
> (Cantor et al., 2019, p311)

A combination of both genetic factors and early experiences shape neuronal connections, which develop neural circuits. These enable increasingly complex mental activities to occur (Moore, 2015; Slavich and Cole, 2013). As these circuits become increasingly stable, they contribute to the development of complex thoughts, skills and behaviours in individuals (Cantor et al., 2019). Environmental and interpersonal experiences influence brain growth throughout childhood and well into adulthood. It has been demonstrated that 'genes act as followers, not prime movers, in developmental processes' (Cantor et al., 2019, p309). It has also been demonstrated that positive, nurturing relationships are essential to brain development. These relationships build strong brain architecture (Cantor et al., 2019). We know that children's development is shaped by micro-ecological contexts (i.e. families, peers, schools and communities) as well as macro-ecological contexts (i.e. economic and cultural systems).

The brain is characterised by plasticity rather than stability. Its structure is influenced not just by genetics, but by the micro and macro contexts within which individuals are situated. Physical, psychological, social and emotional processes also influence brain structure. Emotions can have powerful effects on developmental pathways (Cantor et al., 2019). The implications of this are significant because the research demonstrates that an individual's experiences can shape the development of neural pathways which facilitate mental processes. Thus, exposure to high-quality teaching can change the structure of the brain by activating new neural pathways.

BEHAVIOURIST APPROACHES TO LEARNING

Tabula rasa is a term taken from a Latin phrase that translates as 'smooth or erased tablet'. The term has been used by philosophers to argue that babies are born with mental blankness, where the mind is essentially a blank slate. It is therefore argued here that it is the presence of outside impressions – or stimuli – that support children to acquire knowledge and experiences.

In behaviourist approaches to learning, children respond to stimuli in the environment. Your role as a teacher is to provide engaging and relevant stimuli that children can respond to. This process of engagement and response enables children to gain new knowledge and experience. This approach suggests that appropriate behaviours can therefore be taught by repeatedly exposing children to tasks. This should be combined with positive feedback to recognise and reinforce success and negative feedback to encourage correction and discourage further instances of undesirable behaviour.

In 1927, Ivan Pavlov conducted an experiment in which he taught dogs to salivate when they heard a bell ring (Pavlov, 1927). Pavlov did this by linking feeding time to the bell ringing. When he stopped feeding the dogs in this way, they continued to salivate when the bell was rung. This behaviour had been learned through repeatedly exposing the dogs to a specific sequence of events, and this is therefore an example of a behaviourist approach to learning. Pavlov's discovery is now referred to as classical conditioning. This occurs when behaviours are learned and determined by something that precedes the behaviour – in this case, ringing a bell or making a specific noise. On the other hand, operant conditioning occurs when a behaviour is learned and determined by the anticipation of what follows the behaviour (e.g. a child modifying their behaviour because they are concerned about a sanction or because they are seeking a reward).

CONSTRUCTIVIST APPROACHES TO LEARNING

Jean Piaget was a constructivist. He developed a stage theory to explain cognitive development in children (Piaget, 1936). He believed that learning was promoted through the child's interactions with their natural environment and resources. The stages of his theory are summarised below:

- *Sensorimotor stage (0–2 years).* At this stage, the infant interacts with the world and they begin to realise that they can cause things to happen.

- *Preoperational stage (2–7 years).* Children operating at this stage tend to be egocentric. At this stage, they do not understand the principle of conservation (see below) but will begin to engage in play and learn symbols.

- *Concrete operational stage (7–11 years)*. At this stage, children become less egocentric, but their thinking is very concrete rather than abstract. They begin to understand that other people's views may be different to their views. At this stage, children develop an understanding of conservation (see below) and will be able to develop logical thought.

- *Formal operational stage (12 and above)*. At this stage, children are more able to cope with abstract ideas and abstract problems.

CONSERVATION

Piaget's conservation task is outlined below:

- Children are shown two identical volumes of liquid and two containers. One container is a tall, thin container and the other is a short, fat container.

- One liquid is poured into the tall, thin container and the other liquid is poured into the short, fat container.

- Children are asked, 'Which container has the most?'

- Children at the preoperational stage think that the tall, thin container has the most liquid because it is taller than the other container. They cannot conserve.

- Children at the concrete operational stage know that both containers hold the same amount of liquid even though there appears to be more liquid in the tall, thin container. These children can conserve. They have reached a higher stage of cognitive development.

Another example of a conservation task is outlined below:

- The teacher shows the child two rows of six counters, with the counters in each row lining up with the counters in the other row.

- The teacher asks the child, 'Which row has more?'

- The teacher then spreads the counters on one row out so that the row is longer than the other row, and asks, 'Which row has more?'

- The child who can conserve knows that both rows have the same number of counters, even though one row is longer and therefore appears to have more counters.

- The child who has not yet developed conservation skills thinks that the longer line has more counters because it is longer.

EGOCENTRICITY

Piaget's famous three mountains task demonstrated that children working at earlier stages of cognitive development have an inability to see things from other people's viewpoints. They are egocentric. In the task, a child faced a display of three model mountains. A researcher placed a doll at different positions around the model. The child was asked what the doll could see at each point. Piaget concluded that children working at earlier stages of development could not distinguish between their own view and that of the doll, which Piaget interpreted as evidence of egocentrism (Figure 2.2).

Figure 2.2

BRUNER'S MODEL OF CHILD DEVELOPMENT

Jerome Bruner (1966) proposed that children move through three stages of development:

- enactive representation (action-based);

- iconic representation (image-based);

- symbolic representation (language-based).

At the enactive stage, children learn through physical interactions and movements. At the iconic stage, children learn primarily through visual information, and therefore diagrams, photographs and other images are important in supporting learning at this stage. At the symbolic stage, children learn through symbols such as letters, words and mathematical symbols.

There are similarities between this model and Piaget's theory of cognitive development (Piaget, 1936). We have represented this theory as follows (Figure 2.3).

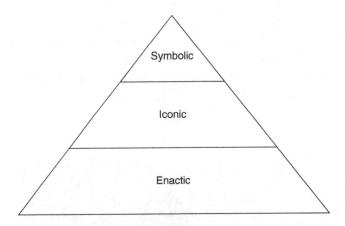

Figure 2.3

The enactive stage lays the foundations for the other two phases. The implications of this are that young children, particularly those in the early years, need rich opportunities to learn through first-hand experiences. They need opportunities to learn through physically interacting with their environment and resources, thus highlighting the importance of play-based pedagogy in the early years. In addition, children at the enactive stage need to learn through exploring concrete resources. Their learning is deepened by having opportunities to use manipulative resources across the curriculum. When children progress to the iconic stage, they can learn through visual resources, including pictures, photographs, diagrams and videos. However, the problem with Bruner's model is that as children progress to more complex and abstract learning, particularly when they reach the symbolic stage, concrete resources and opportunities to learn through first-hand experiences can help children to make sense of abstract concepts. There is a danger that teachers could move children away from active learning too quickly, and we argue that opportunities to learn through physical movement and other forms of first-hand experience are critical at all stages of development.

CRITICISMS OF STAGE THEORIES

Stage theories have been criticised for presenting overly simplistic models of how children develop. Children operate at different stages of development and do not always progress through certain stages at specific ages, as Piaget suggested. In addition, learning is a complex process. Children do not just progress from one stage to another across all subject areas and other domains (e.g. their social, physical and emotional development). In addition, Piaget's work has been criticised for lacking methodological robustness.

SOCIAL CONSTRUCTIVIST APPROACHES TO LEARNING

Vygotsky is one of the most frequently cited scholars associated with social constructivist learning. This approach assumes that social and cultural contexts and language promote learning.

Social constructivist perspectives on learning assume that children's learning and development are promoted within social contexts (Vygotsky, 1978). Vygotsky developed the concept of the zone of proximal development. This is the distance between a child's actual level of development and their proximal level (i.e. what they are capable of achieving with the support from a more able peer or adult). Scaffolding is used to support a child to move between the two stages of development, but learning should always be pitched within the zone so that it is always a level above the child's current level of development. Vygotsky was interested in how dialogue (including internal dialogue and dialogue between individuals) promotes learning within social and cultural contexts.

COLLABORATIVE LEARNING

Research demonstrates that brain development is experience-dependent (Darling-Hammond et al., 2019). Research has also found that cooperative learning promotes higher achievement compared to individualistic efforts (Johnson et al., 2000). The implications for pedagogy are for teachers to provide rich collaborative learning opportunities through paired work and group work. These opportunities may involve learners working together to solve a problem, complete a task or create a new product. When learners are working together on activities or learning tasks, it is important to ensure that groups are small. This ensures that everyone is able to participate and support a collective task that has been clearly assigned. Learners in the group may work on separate tasks that contribute to an overall goal, or they may work together on a shared task. Planning, organising, monitoring and evaluating project-based learning develops pupils' metacognitive skills.

SELF-ESTEEM

Like most psychological concepts, self-esteem it is not straightforward. Self-esteem can act as a buffer which supports individuals to cope with adverse situations (Jindal-Snape and Miller, 2010). Mruk's (1999) two-dimensional model of self-esteem is supported by empirical studies (Tafarodi and Milne, 2002; Tafarodi and Swann, 1995).

The model identifies two components of self-esteem: self-worth and self-competence. According to this model, self-esteem is conceptualised as the integrated sum of these two components (Jindal-Snape and Miller, 2010). Self-worth is an individual's appraisal of themselves based on other people's evaluations of them, and self-competence refers to an individual's sense of their ability to meet the challenges that they face in life (Figure 2.4).

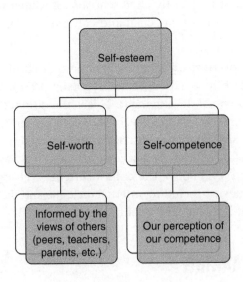

Figure 2.4

When both self-worth and self-competence are positive, self-esteem is high. However, in cases where individuals demonstrate a deficiency on one or both dimensions, they can develop pseudo or defensive self-esteem (Mruk, 1999). Individuals who demonstrate self-worth but not self-competence may develop avoidance strategies when they are asked to complete challenges (Jindal-Snape and Miller, 2010). Those who have low self-worth (due to trauma, a history of receiving negative feedback and other adverse experiences) but a positive sense of competence may demonstrate antisocial behaviours. If both constructs are deficient, overall self-esteem is likely to be low. The model is demarcated into quadrants, and individuals may fall into any one of the quadrants (Figure 2.5).

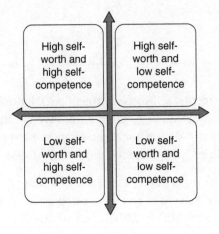

Figure 2.5

Jan Stets and Peter Burke have identified three components of self-esteem: self-worth, self-efficacy and authenticity. The verification of personal identities, either by the self or by others, enables individuals to acknowledge and live out their 'true' self: 'They are being who they "really" are at their core and others are confirming this' (Stets and Burke, 2014, p8) (Figure 2.6).

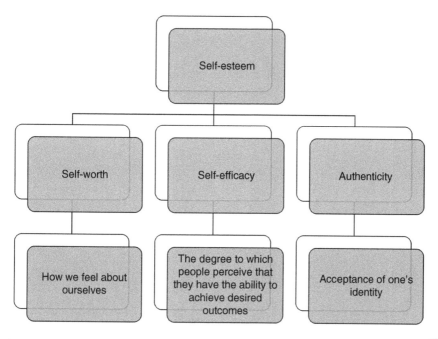

Figure 2.6

RESILIENCE

Earlier perspectives on resilience conceptualised it as a fixed trait within individuals (Masten and Garmezy, 1985). However, contemporary perspectives tend to conceptualise resilience as a dynamic attribute that can be enhanced (Luthar, 2006; Roffey, 2017; Stephens, 2013). Definitions of resilience emphasise positive adaptation following adversity or trauma (Gayton and Lovell, 2012) and the capacity to grow in response to adversity (Stallman, 2011). Definitions capture the capacity to rebound from adversity, to problem-solve and to return to the previous state (Sanderson and Brewer, 2017). This ability to 'push through' regardless of circumstances is a dominant theme in the literature (Reyes et al., 2015), but these perspectives only offer a partial understanding of resilience.

We conceptualise resilience as a dynamic characteristic. Our capacity to be resilient across contexts is dependent upon access to social networks and emotional support from others within our ecosystems. It is influenced by the nature of the challenges that individuals are exposed to as well as the wider context. Our conceptualisation of resilience is presented in the following model (Figure 2.7).

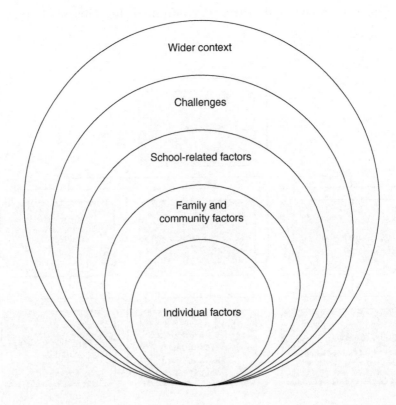

Figure 2.7

- *Individual factors*. Resilience is affected by an individual's sense of purpose, hope and self-efficacy.

- *Family and community factors*. Access to supportive, nurturing and loving relationships that are underpinned by secure attachments impact positively on resilience.

- *School factors*. Positive school cultures and positive relationships with teachers enable individuals to be more resilient.

- *Challenges*. The extent of the challenges that individuals face influences their capacity to be resilient. Experience of trauma can have a long-lasting, detrimental impact on resilience.

- *Wider context*. Policy/legislation that protects people's rights can impact on resilience. Broader economic, political, cultural and social contexts influence people's lives and can impact on resilience.

PROMOTING A GROWTH MINDSET: BRAIN DEVELOPMENT

Research demonstrates that the brain can physically change and that this can occur well into adulthood (Abiola and Dhindsa, 2012). Research undertaken by Maguire et al. (2006) examined the physical changes in the brain in individuals undertaking training to become London taxi drivers. The research demonstrated that following the training, there was a significant growth in the hippocampus, the area of the brain that processes spatial information (Maguire et al., 2006). Research that demonstrates the plasticity of the brain supports the belief that intellectual ability can be enhanced and developed through learning (Sternberg, 2005). It therefore supports the idea of a 'growth mindset' (Dweck, 1999). People with growth mindsets believe that intelligence can grow and be developed through effort. In contrast, those with fixed mindsets view intelligence as a static trait and not something that can be developed.

Dweck (2007, 2009) argued that mindsets play a critical role in the motivation and achievement of learners. Learners with a fixed mindset can easily give up when learning becomes too challenging. Conversely, learners with a growth mindset embrace learning opportunities that provide challenge, even where failure is a very real possibility (Dweck, 2007). Although two individuals with differing mindsets can start out achieving similar levels academically, research suggests that over time the individual with the growth mindset will begin to outperform the individual with the fixed mindset (Dweck, 2009). Research demonstrates that 'at every socioeconomic level, those who hold more of a growth mindset consistently outperform those who do not' (Claro et al., 2016, p4).

Fixed-ability thinking can encourage inequality (Boaler, 2013) because individuals with fixed mindsets may lack motivation and resilience and may not be prepared to invest effort into developing their brains. In the worst cases, these individuals give up on learning and develop 'learned helplessness'.

The attitudes of teachers towards intelligence and school culture play an important role in how students view themselves. The use of ability groupings in schools promotes the idea of a fixed mindset. Boaler (2013) has argued that ability groupings transmit to students the view that some students are not capable of completing more challenging tasks, thus suggesting that intelligence is static. Static groups are common in schools; the opportunity to change groups is limited (Davies et al., 2003; Dixon, 2002) and research suggests that most pupils remain in the same ability group for the duration of their school careers (Ollerton, 2001). This promotes the idea of a fixed mindset, which is transmitted to students.

Dweck (2010) suggests that the culture and learning approaches within schools could help students to change their approach to learning and encourage the development of growth mindset beliefs. A shift in culture may require teachers to reframe their perceptions of intelligence and for schools to review the use of fixed-ability groups.

TAKE 5

- Environmental factors can influence the structure of the brain.

- The brain is malleable rather than static, and good teaching can promote brain growth and intelligence.

- Intelligence is not fixed.

- Children need opportunities to interact with resources individually to 'construct' their own knowledge (constructivism).

- Children require opportunities to learn through social and language-rich contexts (social constructivism).

CLASSROOM EXAMPLE

A Year 6 teacher wanted to use social constructivist approaches to learning in her classroom. She asked the children to work in groups to create a mini enterprise. The children had to decide on a company that they wanted to create, as well as naming the company and developing a product. Each group had to work together to design a product. They first had to generate ideas and then conduct market research by testing out these ideas with potential customers and gaining feedback. Following this, they modified their original ideas. They worked as a group to make the product, as well as marketing and selling it. Different people took responsibility for different roles, and sometimes the roles were rotated so that children had the opportunity to develop different skills. This project developed metacognitive skills, particularly in relation to identifying goals, planning, monitoring and evaluating.

WHAT DOES GOOD PRACTICE IN PROMOTING LEARNING LOOK LIKE IN THE CLASSROOM?

A primary teacher used constructivist approaches in science. The children were learning about bar magnets. With no direct teaching, the teacher provided the children with bar magnets and asked them to explore what happened when they put these together. The children realised that like poles repelled and opposite poles attracted.

In the next lesson, the teacher provided them with magnets and a range of metals. She started the lesson by asking them to predict whether the metals would or would not be attracted to the magnets. She also gave them a variety of different materials, including plastic, wood, card and fabric, and asked them to predict if the materials would or would not be attracted to the magnets. The children all predicted that all the metals would be attracted to the magnets. They were then given time to explore the materials and the magnets. To their surprise, the children discovered that most of the metals were not attracted to the magnets, but that iron was attracted to the magnets. This moved their learning through their zone of proximal development.

In an early years classroom, the children were given lots of opportunities to learn through constructivist approaches. Resources were left available for them on interactive displays so that they could learn about light. They had access to torches and coloured acetates so that they could experiment with changing the colour of the light. In the water tray, a variety of objects was made available so that the children could investigate which floated and which sank. The children had free access to mathematical shapes, rulers, cubes and counters in the maths area to support the development of their mathematical knowledge. In the reading area, the children had access to printed versions of books and digital books on electronic tablets. The children could move freely between indoor and outdoor learning. In the outdoor area, they had opportunities to investigate minibeasts in the garden, create dens, and develop problem-solving skills through building structures using tyres, rope, cardboard boxes and crates.

Children in Year 2 were learning about the working lives of children in Victorian Britain. The teacher wanted them to imagine what life would have been like for children who had to work down the mines. She decided to do a drama lesson in which the children had to create dens using blackout sheeting draped over tables. In small groups, the children created dens. She asked them to go inside their dens to experience life in total darkness. She asked them to generate vocabulary to describe how they felt. The children generated a wide range of vocabulary, including 'terrified', 'anxious', 'nervous', 'frightened', 'scared' and 'lonely'. In a subsequent writing lesson, the teacher asked the class to write a description of life as a child miner. She asked them to recall the vocabulary they had used in the drama lesson. The experience of being in the 'mine' and the immersion in oral language in the drama lesson had a powerful effect on the children's writing. The children used the rich vocabulary from the drama lesson in their writing. This example highlights the powerful role of language in the learning process.

CHAPTER CHECKLIST

	Accessed	Secure	Confident
Know that:			
several theories inform our understanding of children's development and learning			

(Continued)

(Continued)

	Accessed	Secure	Confident
Know how to:			
use constructivist approaches to support learning			
use social constructivist approaches to support learning			
use behaviourist approaches to support learning			
develop children's metacognitive skills			

3

MEMORY

┌─ **IN THIS CHAPTER** ────────────────────────────────

In this chapter, you will learn about working memory and long-term memory. You will also learn about the different components of both memory types. The development of schemas and cognitive load is also addressed. Memory is critical to the learning process. Information transfers from the working memory into the long-term memory but our capacity to retrieve information is essential. Information can be stored in the long-term memory for many years or even a lifetime, but retrieval brings that information to the forefront.

KEY RESEARCH

As Kirschner et al. (2006) point out, 'If nothing has changed in long-term memory, nothing has been learned' (p77). Research suggests that an effective approach to curriculum planning is to revisit learning and repeat practice over time, as this leads to better long-term retention of knowledge (Rawson and Kintsch, 2005). Reviewing previous learning leads to much greater long-term retention if subject content is spread out, with gaps in between to allow students to forget the content (Coe et al., 2014). This 'is one of the most general and robust effects from across the entire history of experimental research on learning and memory' (Bjork and Bjork, 2011, p59). Many students benefit from repeated exposure to subject content, particularly when content is spaced out and revisited rather than taught in a single block and never revisited.

KEY POLICY

The early career framework states that teachers must learn:

- Working memory is where information that is being actively processed is held, but its capacity is limited and can be overloaded.

- Long-term memory can be considered as a store of knowledge that changes as pupils learn by integrating new ideas with existing knowledge.

(DfE, 2019a)

WHAT IS MEMORY?

'Memory is the term given to the structures and processes involved in the storage and subsequent retrieval of information' (McLeod, 2013). The development of memory is critical to learning. There are two *main* types of memory: working memory and long-term memory. The working memory holds a limited amount of information that is used to execute cognitive tasks. It enables individuals to hold multiple pieces of information that are used to complete a variety of daily tasks. In contrast, the long-term memory stores information indefinitely, including information that is not being used in the working memory. Repetition is required to 'fix' information in the long-term memory, but once it is stored in the long-term memory it can remain there for a significant time.

THE WORKING MEMORY MODEL

The working memory is the part of the memory that enables us to complete tasks. Baddeley and Hitch (1974) proposed a model of working memory in an attempt to describe a more accurate model of short-term memory. The working memory model is composed of three main components: the 'central executive', which acts as the main system and controls the flow of information to and from its 'slave systems' – the 'phonological loop' and the 'visuospatial sketch pad'. The slave systems are short-term storage systems. Each is dedicated to a content domain (verbal and visuospatial, respectively).

Thus, the components of working memory include:

- *Central executive.* This drives the working memory and the subsystems of working memory: the phonological loop and the visuospatial sketch pad. It also deals with cognitive tasks.

- *Phonological loop.* This is the part of working memory that deals with spoken and written material. This is a slave system of the central executive.

- *Visuospatial sketch pad.* This stores and processes information in a visual or spatial form, and is therefore essential for navigation. This is a slave system of the central executive.

- *Episodic buffer.* This is a temporary storage system that combines information from the phonological loop and the visuospatial sketch pad. It also communicates with the long-term memory.

The model is represented visually as follows (Figure 3.1).

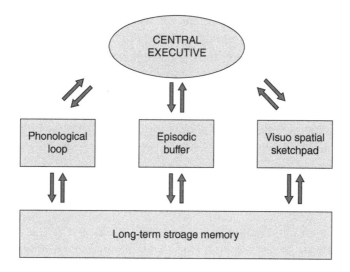

Figure 3.1

The working memory is an active, temporary memory system that enables us to store information while we are completing a task. It holds multiple pieces of information, but its capacity is limited to approximately seven pieces of information.

THE PHONOLOGICAL LOOP

This is represented in the following diagram (Figure 3.2).

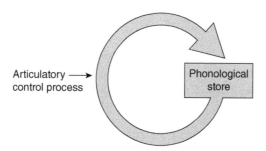

Figure 3.2

The phonological loop is a component of the working memory model that processes auditory information. It maintains information that is presented as an auditory code. It is subdivided into the phonological store, which holds the information that we hear, and the articulatory process, which enables us to rehearse words that are in the phonological store. Spoken information enters the phonological store directly. Written information must be converted into sound before it can enter the phonological store. The articulatory control process converts written information such as words and numbers into an articulatory code and transfers them to the phonological store. The process operates as a loop because if we keep repeating auditory information, the information is retained in the working memory. If you are trying to memorise your mobile phone number, the process of repeating it transfers the number into the phonological store and into the working memory.

VISUOSPATIAL SKETCH PAD

The visuospatial sketch pad enables us to store visual and spatial information. It is sub-divided into a visual store and a spatial store, which together support visual and spatial processing. It is the part of the working memory that is responsible for spatial awareness and navigation. If you are trying to remember the route to a particular building on a university campus, this is the part of the memory that you are activating. If you are trying to find your car in a large car park, you are processing this task visually (looking for the colour of your car) but also spatially (remembering the route to your car). The visuospatial sketch pad is an active component of the working memory.

EPISODIC BUFFER

The episodic buffer was added later to the model by Baddeley (2000). It is a temporary store that combines information from the phonological loop, the visuospatial sketch pad and the long-term memory. It enables information from these stores to be held temporarily and combines the information under the control of the central executive. If you are completing a task that combines visual, spatial and auditory information, you are drawing on both of the slave systems of the working memory (i.e. the phonological loop and the visuospatial sketch pad).

KEY FACTS ABOUT THE WORKING MEMORY

- The phonological loop allows us to remember auditory information through the process of repetition (e.g. learning a telephone number by repeating it).

- Information that enters the phonological loop as an auditory code is transferred into the phonological store.

- Information that enters the phonological loop as a visual code (e.g. a written word) has to be converted to an auditory code before it can enter the phonological store.

- The visuospatial sketch pad allows us to store visual and spatial information.

- Both the phonological loop and the visuospatial sketch pad are slave systems of the central executive.

- Tasks that interfere with each other cause cognitive overload. This happens when tasks use the same component of the working memory. An example of this is when we try to learn a set of letters while counting backwards in threes from 100. Both tasks require the phonological loop and therefore interfere with each other.

- The working memory can cope with more than one task provided that different components of the working memory are used (e.g. completing an auditory task at the same time as completing a task that requires the retrieval of visual or spatial information from the sketch pad). The episodic buffer will combine the information from both slave systems to enable this task to be completed.

- Serial processing is when a component of the working memory completes one task before completing another.

- Parallel processing is when both slave systems (i.e. the phonological loop and the visuospatial sketch pad) complete tasks at the same time.

LONG-TERM MEMORY

We can store information in the long-term memory for a few minutes, long periods of time, or sometimes even for a lifetime. It has unlimited capacity. However, our capacity to retrieve information influences whether we can recall the information that the long-term memory holds. It includes:

- *Semantic memory.* This is the part of the long-term memory responsible for storing information about the world. This includes knowledge about the meaning of words, as well as general knowledge.

- *Episodic memory.* This is the part of the long-term memory responsible for storing information about events (i.e. episodes) that we have experienced in our lives.

- *Procedural memory.* This is the aspect of our memory that helps us to remember how to do things (e.g. how to fasten a knot in a tie or how to tie our shoelaces).

INFORMATION PROCESSING

Memory covers three important aspects of information processing:

- memory encoding;

- memory storage;

- memory retrieval.

MEMORY ENCODING

When information comes into our memory system through our senses, it needs to be changed into a form that the system can cope with so that it can be stored. This process is known as encoding. For example, a word that is seen (in a book) may be stored if it is changed (encoded) into a sound or a meaning (i.e. semantic processing).

For example, children can remember a word that they have read in a book (visual processing) by changing the word into a sound (auditory processing). They may code the word in their memory by sound. In addition, children may attach a meaning to the word (semantic processing). The memory therefore uses the following types of coding when information comes into the memory:

- visual;

- acoustic;

- semantic.

Evidence suggests that acoustic coding is the principle coding system in the working memory (McLeod, 2013). We remember information by rehearsing the information verbally. Think back to when you were at school and you had to remember the first 20 elements in the periodic table in science. It is likely that you repeated them verbally. They are converted from visual information to auditory information in the working memory. Think about how you remember a telephone number. It is likely that you convert it from visual information to auditory information by repeating it several times. The telephone number then goes into your memory as an acoustic code rather than a visual code. Research suggests that the principle encoding system in long-term memory appears to be semantic coding (by meaning) (McLeod, 2013). We attach meanings to the information that enters the long-term memory. However, information in the long-term memory can also be coded acoustically and visually.

MEMORY STORAGE

Memory storage concerns the nature of memory stores – i.e. where the information is stored, how long the memory lasts for (duration), how much can be stored at any time (capacity), and what kind of information is held (McLeod, 2013).

Research suggests that most adults can store between five and nine items in their working memory (McLeod, 2013). Miller (1956) proposed that individuals were capable of storing seven items of information (or memory 'slots') in the working memory. However, it is possible to group pieces of information together so that several pieces of information can fit into each slot, which then increases the amount of information that can be stored in the working memory. Information can only be stored in the working memory for a limited amount of time.

The short-term memory stores small amounts of information for short periods of time with relatively little processing. It is a single store without any subsystems. In contrast, working memory is not a unitary store. It can hold multiple pieces of information.

MEMORY RETRIEVAL

This is the process of retrieving information from storage. If we cannot remember something, it may be because we are unable to retrieve it from the memory. If information is stored sequentially, then this process aids retrieval. For this reason, it is important to consider carefully how to sequence subject-specific content in teaching. If teachers spend time thinking about how to sequence subject-specific knowledge, concepts and skills, this will mean that information can be stored sequentially in the memory. This will support memory retrieval.

COGNITIVE LOAD

Cognitive load theory addresses techniques for managing working memory load in order to enable learners to process complex cognitive tasks (Paas et al., 2003). The aim is to reduce the load on the working memory so that it can function more efficiently. If a single slave system of the working memory is attempting to complete two tasks at the same time, the tasks will conflict with each other, resulting in cognitive overload. Each slave system can complete a task in parallel at the same time, and the tasks will not conflict because each task is being completed using a separate component of the working memory. Teachers can reduce the load on the working memory by breaking down or 'chunking' information in manageable ways and by connecting new learning to previous learning. Research has also found that cognitive load in the classroom is exacerbated by adverse experiences that students are exposed to (Darling-Hammond et al., 2019) because they are actively processing those experiences as well as processing tasks in the classroom.

SCHEMAS

One of the ways in which the brain stores information is through the development of schemas. Schemas are mental structures of frameworks for representing some aspect of the world, including knowledge. Organising knowledge into schemas facilitates its retrieval from the long-term memory. Schemas can be considered to be categories that a child develops through their interactions with the world and with others.

Schemas are coherent mental representations of subject content that are stored in the long-term memory.

Developing accurate schemas is important to help students understand how subject-specific content is connected, but it also ensures that information can be easily retrieved from the long-term memory. Think of it as being similar to a filing cabinet or the folders of information on a computer.

For example
A child may develop a schema about cars. They learn that cars have four wheels and a steering wheel and they apply this schema to identify cars when they see one.

Schemas are coherent mental representations of subject content that are stored in the long-term memory. Developing accurate schemas is important to help students understand how subject-specific content is connected, but it also ensures that information can be easily retrieved from the long-term memory. Think of it as being similar to a filing cabinet or the folders of information on a computer.

Explicit guided teaching ensures that students develop accurate schemas. Constructivist theory shifts the emphasis away from teaching a subject as a body of knowledge, and instead emphasises learning a subject by experiencing the processes and procedures of the subject (Handelsman et al., 2004).

A child may develop a schema about cars. They learn that cars have four wheels and a steering wheel, and they apply this schema to identify cars when they see one. Schemas continue to develop throughout childhood and into adult life. They are convenient categories for storing information to aid retrieval. One way of thinking about them is to imagine they are storage folders that group together information which fits into a specific category.

Piaget articulated how new learning occurs using schemas (Piaget and Cook, 1952). He used the term 'assimilation' when new information is added to current schemas. In the example above, the child's existing schema (i.e. that a car has four wheels and a steering wheel) is applied to different sizes, colours and makes of car. The schema still works because the different models are all cars. Piaget referred to this as a process of 'equilibrium'. However, 'disequilibrium' occurs when new information cannot be fitted into existing schemas. This causes the child to experience what Piaget referred to as 'cognitive dissonance'. This is where schemas are forced to change to 'accommodate' new information. This happens when the existing schema (knowledge) does not work and needs to be changed to deal with a new object or situation. In the same example, the child may see a bus and call it a car but then subsequently learn that this is incorrect. The schema no longer works and needs to be changed. The process of reframing a schema can be challenging, but this is when learning occurs. It is the process through which new knowledge is accommodated with existing knowledge to return to a state of equilibrium. The processes of equilibrium and disequilibrium then continue as schemas become increasingly more complex.

TAKE 5

- The working memory can hold multiple pieces of information but it can only store them for a limited time.

- The long-term memory can hold information for a few minutes, months or even years, but that information must be retrieved.

- Children with poor retrieval capacity may struggle to recall subject-specific knowledge, concepts and skills.

(Continued)

(Continued)

- Children with good retrieval capacity can recall the information they have been taught.
- Memory can be strengthened.

CLASSROOM EXAMPLE

In Year 1, a group of children are struggling to remember the phonemes when they are shown specific graphemes. The teacher uses a range of approaches to support the children to remember the phonemes:

- The teacher shows the children one grapheme and enunciates the phoneme. The children repeat the phoneme and demonstrate the action that represents the phoneme which the teacher has demonstrated to them.

- The teacher uses the strategy of 'overlearning'. The above activity is repeated several times a day, for several days or even several weeks.

- Once the children have mastered one grapheme–phoneme correspondence (GPC), the teacher introduces them to another GPC.

- The children work on learning a small selection of GPCs. These are repeated frequently.

- The children trace the grapheme in the air at the same time as enunciating the phoneme.

- The children trace their fingers over graphemes made from sandpaper at the same time as enunciating the phoneme.

- The children are given opportunities to trace these graphemes in sand, glitter, soil and coloured rice.

- The children are asked to paint the graphemes that they are learning or to draw them with chalks.

- The children trace the graphemes on the palms of their hands at the same time as enunciating the phonemes.

- The children trace over the wooden letters to experience the shape of the grapheme while concurrently enunciating the phoneme.

These activities provide the children with a rich range of multisensory experiences. However, it is the combination of visual, auditory and kinaesthetic approaches that helps the children to say the phonemes automatically when they see the graphemes. This multisensory approach helps to 'fix' the information into the child's memory.

WHAT DOES GOOD PRACTICE IN SUPPORTING MEMORY LOOK LIKE IN THE CLASSROOM?

Some children with poor memories may struggle to recall subject-specific knowledge, concepts and skills in a range of subjects. However, the following activities can strengthen memory:

- Show the children two objects (e.g. an apple and a banana). Ask them to look at the objects and to remember them. Ask them to close their eyes. Hide one of the objects. Ask them to open their eyes and identify which object has been removed.

- Repeat the above with three objects and remove one object.

- Repeat this with four, five and six objects and remove one.

- This process can be continued over time, gradually extending the number of objects.

- When they are confident, start removing two objects.

- Then extend the number of objects and remove three objects.

This activity helps to develop the memory. The activity could be adapted by using a soft toy that is dressed. Remove one item of clothing, then two, then three. These memory games support children to hold information in their memories.

CHAPTER CHECKLIST

	Accessed	Secure	Confident
Know that:			
theories and models of memory inform practice			
Know how to:			
plan learning sequences to take account of cognitive load			
use retrieval practices			
use multisensory approaches to strengthen memory			
structure tasks to reduce overload on the working memory			

4

SUBJECT KNOWLEDGE

— IN THIS CHAPTER

This chapter introduces you to key research on the importance of good and deep subject knowledge. It outlines the three key aspects of subject knowledge and how these contribute to teaching and learning, and therefore children's outcomes. Throughout the chapter, practical guidance is offered to support you to impart knowledge effectively and foster pupils' interest in your subject. The chapter also presents research in relation to systematic synthetic phonics. In doing so, it argues there is no conclusive evidence that one form of phonics is superior to another. It emphasises the importance of a systematic approach to phonics and that one approach does not necessarily meet the needs of all children.

KEY RESEARCH

The most effective teachers have deep knowledge of the subjects they teach, and when teachers' knowledge falls below a certain level it is a significant impediment to students' learning. As well as a strong understanding of the material being taught, teachers must also understand the ways students think about the content, be able to evaluate the thinking behind students' own methods and identify students' common misconceptions.

(Coe et al., 2014, p2)

KEY POLICY

The teachers' standards state that teachers must:

- have a secure knowledge of the relevant subject(s) and curriculum areas, foster and maintain pupils' interest in the subject, and address misunderstandings;

- demonstrate a critical understanding of developments in the subject and curriculum areas, and promote the value of scholarship;

- demonstrate an understanding of and take responsibility for promoting high standards of literacy, articulacy and the correct use of standard English, whatever the teacher's specialist subjects;

- if teaching early reading, demonstrate a clear understanding of systematic synthetic phonics;

- if teaching early mathematics, demonstrate a clear understanding of appropriate teaching strategies.

(DfE, 2011)

WHAT IS SUBJECT KNOWLEDGE?

The Training and Development Agency for Schools (TDA) developed a model that showed three components of subject knowledge (TDA, 2007). According to the model, subject knowledge for teaching is made up of the following aspects (Figure 4.1):

- subject knowledge per se (i.e. your knowledge of the subject content – its concepts, facts, theories and skills);

- pedagogical subject knowledge;

- pupils' development.

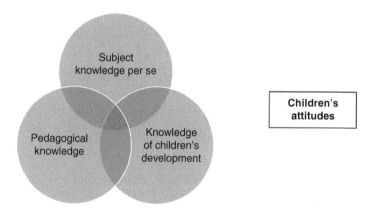

Figure 4.1

Pupils' attitudes sit around the outside of the model because they influence all the other components. Knowing how to motivate, enthuse and engage pupils within specific subjects is essential, and will support pupils' development within the subject.

SUBJECT KNOWLEDGE PER SE

Your knowledge of the subject content is critical to effective teaching and outcomes for children. Strong subject knowledge will give you confidence to explain things clearly, answer children's questions, and address their misconceptions. Having a strong grasp of the subject content will also enable you to provide suitable learning challenges for children who are operating at higher stages of development.

Making decisions about how to sequence subject content across a sequence of lessons requires you to understand how knowledge, skills and understanding progress across a unit of work. Having a secure knowledge of subject progression will enable you to address misconceptions and to challenge children further.

Subject knowledge per se includes:

- the key concepts, language, skills and topics that define the subject area;

- progression in the subject.

PEDAGOGICAL SUBJECT KNOWLEDGE

Knowing a subject and understanding the steps that pupils need to make to learn the subject content are not enough in themselves. You also need to develop your knowledge of how to teach that subject content to enable pupils to learn it. You need to understand the subject-specific knowledge, concepts and skills. You also need to know how to sequence these in a logical way so that they make sense to children when they need them. You therefore need to know how to sequence subject-specific content across a series of lessons so that subsequent learning naturally builds on prior learning.

Pedagogical subject knowledge includes:

- a range of teaching skills and strategies to promote pupils' learning in the subject;

- the ability to plan lessons and sequences of lessons;

- the use of approaches for subject-specific assessment.

PUPILS' DEVELOPMENT

Understanding how pupils develop their knowledge and understanding of a subject is an essential component of good subject knowledge. Also, it is important to understand a range of factors that affect pupils' learning and how to adapt subject-specific approaches to meet the needs of pupils working at different stages of development.

EARLY MATHEMATICS

Children learn initially through concrete representations before progressing to abstract representations and abstract thinking. Young children may require access to manipulative objects

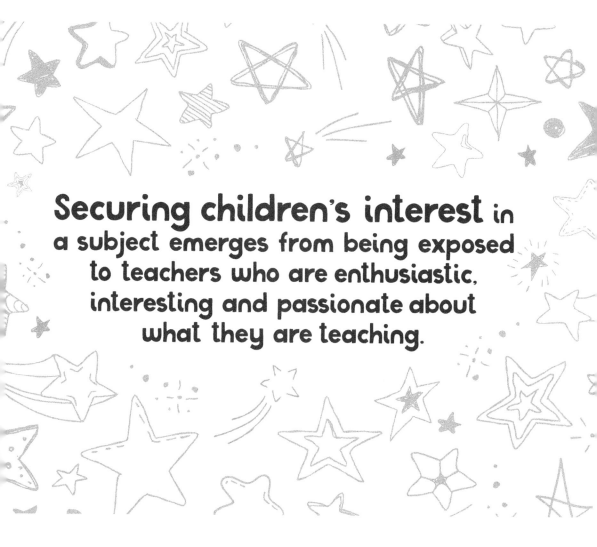

Securing children's interest in a subject emerges from being exposed to teachers who are enthusiastic, interesting and passionate about what they are teaching.

and visual forms of representation to support them in their learning. Providing children with concrete representations is an effective way of supporting their subject-specific understanding. As children learn, they move from concrete representations to abstract thinking. Concrete representations in mathematics include a variety of practical manipulative resources, including counters, blocks and place value apparatus. Children initially rely on these resources to develop their understanding of specific mathematical concepts and skills. They progress from concrete resources to visual representations. An example is where a child moves from using counters or blocks to support addition to using visual representations (e.g. drawings or working out on paper). Eventually, the child can learn in a more abstract way. In this example, the child may start to use a variety of mental methods to solve addition problems.

FOSTERING PUPILS' INTEREST IN YOUR SUBJECT

Securing children's interest in a subject emerges from being exposed to teachers who are enthusiastic, interesting and passionate about what they are teaching. The best teachers can make even very 'dry' content interesting. The following strategies should support you in fostering pupils' interest in subject content:

- Plan a 'hook' at the start of the lesson to get their attention.

- Break the lesson up into a series of cumulative stages, setting short, sharp and snappy tasks for children at each stage.

- Provide frequent opportunities for active learning and for children to learn through first-hand experiences.

- Provide opportunities for children to work in pairs.

- Provide opportunities for children to work in small groups.

- Provide opportunities to develop oracy through all subjects.

- Use drama as a pedagogical tool where this is appropriate.

ADDRESSING MISCONCEPTIONS

Children may develop misconceptions in specific aspects of subject content. Your role as a teacher is to unpick these misconceptions with them, explain to them why these have developed, and support them to develop accurate knowledge and understanding.

The best way of addressing misconceptions is to research possible misconceptions that children may develop when you are planning lessons. This will then enable you to explicitly highlight these common misconceptions in your lessons, thus drawing attention to them, and teaching children to avoid developing them in the first place.

Understanding common misconceptions within a subject and supporting pupils to overcome these requires you to have strong subject knowledge. You will also need to ensure that you do not accidently teach the children misconceptions, unless you are drawing their attention to them so that they do not develop them!

You will need to address misconceptions at various stages in a lesson. These include:

- when children answer questions and demonstrate misconceptions through their answers;

- when children are working on a task and you notice them developing misconceptions;

- when you observe children's responses to an assessment for learning task and notice that they have developed misconceptions.

DEVELOPMENTS IN YOUR SUBJECT

You should keep abreast of developments within your subject. Outstanding trainees continue to keep abreast of subject development through:

- engaging in professional discussions with colleagues;

- observing other teachers;

- joining subject associations (e.g. Geographical Association or Historical Association);

- keeping up to date with the latest research;

- joining online communities of teachers.

PROMOTING HIGH STANDARDS OF LITERACY

All teachers are teachers of literacy. You should therefore model accurate spelling, grammar and sentence structure when you are modelling writing for children. It is good practice to have subject-specific vocabulary on display in lessons. It is also good practice to live-model writing in the foundation subjects as well as in English. This will help to ensure high-quality writing across the curriculum. You should take care to ensure that you use standard spoken English when communicating with children.

SYSTEMATIC SYNTHETIC PHONICS

The term 'synthetic' is taken from the verb 'to synthesise'. Synthetic phonics involves the process of breaking a word down into its smallest units of sound (phonemes) and merging these together sequentially for reading. This process is known as decoding or blending. In addition, it also includes the reverse process of separating a word into its constituent phonemes and representing these as graphemes for spelling. This process is known as segmenting. A systematic approach to phonics means that the phonemes and graphemes are taught in a specific order and that there is fidelity to one specific progression sequence.

Synthetic phonics was first promoted by Jim Rose in his *Independent Review of the Teaching of Early Reading* (Rose, 2006). Rose cited an influential study that was conducted in Clackmannanshire (Johnson and Watson, 2004). This study compared the word reading skills of children who were taught synthetic phonics to those who were taught by other approaches. The study found that the children who were taught synthetic phonics made greater gains in word reading than those who were taught using different approaches. However, Johnson and Watson's study had methodological weaknesses, many of which have been documented in previous literature. The study design was not methodologically robust enough for large-scale policy to be implemented on the back of it (for a comprehensive critique of this study, see Glazzard, 2017).

According to Torgerson et al. (2006), 'There is currently no strong randomised controlled trial evidence that any one form of systematic phonics is more effective than any other' (p49). The available evidence is insufficient to allow for reliable judgements to be made about the efficiency of different approaches to phonics instruction (Stuart, 2006). In countries where there are consistent one-to-one mappings between graphemes and phonemes (such as in Finland, Greece, Italy and Spain), evidence suggests that synthetic phonics is effective (Landerl, 2000). However, the English language is not orthographically consistent. This means that there is a need for direct instruction at varying grain sizes in order to develop accurate and automatic word recognition (Goswami, 2005; Wyse and Goswami, 2008). The irregularities of the English language inhibit the effectiveness of synthetic phonics because grapheme–phoneme correspondences (GPCs) are inconsistent (Seymour et al., 2003). Research suggests that children 'code-switch' from small to large grain sizes when they are reading (Brown and Deavers, 1999; Goswami et al., 2003). Some words must be learned as wholes because they are phonically irregular. Some words include rimes, which are generally more consistent than phonemes. Some words can be broken down into constituent phonemes. Teaching a range of grain sizes rather than focusing solely on the level of the phoneme will therefore support more accurate word recognition.

Evidence suggests that no single method of teaching children to read is superior to any other (Landerl, 2000; Spencer and Hanley, 2003; Torgerson et al., 2006; Walton et al., 2001). There is no empirical evidence to justify Rose's recommendation that the teaching of reading in England should rely on synthetic phonics, given the methodological weaknesses that have been identified in relation to the Clackmannanshire study (Wyse and Goswami, 2008; Wyse and Styles, 2007). However, there is clear evidence that a systematic approach to phonics produces gains in word reading and spelling (Torgerson et al., 2006) irrespective of the types of phonics that are taught. Evidence suggests that as long as reading instruction is systematic, this leads to similar gains in word reading (Landerl, 2000; Spencer and Hanley, 2003; Torgerson et al., 2006; Walton et al., 2001) regardless of the types of phonics being taught.

THE SIMPLE VIEW OF READING (SVOR)

The SVOR is a theoretical model for explaining reading development in children (Gough and Tunmer, 1986). The model is shown below (Figure 4.2).

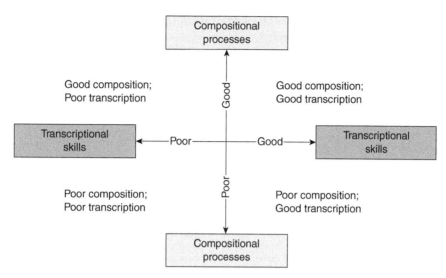

Figure 4.2   A simple view of writing

Bevilacqua and Fenton (2009) Powerpoint presentation

The model demonstrates that the process of reading is the product of both word recognition and language comprehension. To become good readers, children must be able to recognise the words on a page (word recognition) as well as understand language (language comprehension). Without an adequate understanding of language, children will not be able to comprehend the vocabulary in spoken or written language. However, without the skill of word recognition, children will not be able to understand the meanings of the texts that they read.

The model demonstrates that the two skills are separate but that both are essential to becoming an effective reader. Children in the top-right quadrant are skilled in both word recognition and language comprehension. They are effective readers. Those in the bottom-right quadrant are skilled in word recognition but have underdeveloped language comprehension skills. That is, they can read the words on a page but they struggle to understand them. These children are often described as 'barking' at print. Those in the top-left quadrant have good language comprehension skills but struggle with recognising words on a page. These children tend to struggle with the skill of blending phonemes for reading but they often have very good comprehension skills, particularly when they listen to texts that are read to them. Children with dyslexia might fall into this category. Children in the bottom-right quadrant are poor in both word recognition and language comprehension. These children need urgent intervention in both aspects.

The model is useful to teachers for two reasons. First, it can be used as an assessment tool to plot which quadrant children fall into. Teachers can assess each of the separate dimensions (word recognition and language comprehension), and this will then inform what type of intervention is required (i.e. whether they need a word recognition intervention or a language comprehension intervention). Second, the separation of the two skills in the model suggests to teachers that different approaches to teaching are required to develop each of these skills. To develop word recognition, children need to develop their skills in recognising and enunciating phonemes in response to graphemes (grapheme–phoneme correspondences) and they need to blend (synthesise) these phonemes together to read the target word. They also need to recognise exception words. These are words that are not phonetically decodable and may need to be learned by sight. To develop language comprehension, children need access to a rich language environment that exposes them to a breadth of vocabulary. Play-based learning in the early years therefore supports reading development. In addition, children need to learn reading comprehension strategies by developing skills such as prediction, extracting relevant information from texts to answer questions, and the skills of inference and deduction.

TAKE 5

- Immerse children in a language-rich environment.

- Teach word recognition using phonics and whole-word recognition.

- Use concrete resources such as manipulatives in the early stages of development.

- Join subject associations to develop your subject knowledge.

- Sequence subject-specific knowledge, concepts and skills logically so that subsequent learning builds on prior learning.

CLASSROOM EXAMPLE

When children provide an incorrect answer, it is important to establish the reasons underpinning their response before you attempt to elicit a correct answer through scaffolding. It may appear straightforward to ask a child to select the largest number out of a choice of two (e.g. 5.59 and 9.2). If a child identifies 5.59 as the largest number – after comparing 559 and 92 – it is important to address and tackle any misconceptions in relation to decimals and decimal places. This must take place before you provide the correct answer and move on.

WHAT DOES GOOD PRACTICE IN SUBJECT KNOWLEDGE LOOK LIKE IN THE CLASSROOM?

Try to develop links with neighbouring primary schools to share good practice and capitalise on local subject expertise. It is also important to take advantage of subject-specific opportunities for continuing professional development, as well as ensuring that the structure of school staffing supports subject experts to train other staff.

CHAPTER CHECKLIST

	Accessed	Secure	Confident
Know that:			
each subject has distinct knowledge, concepts and skills that I need to know			
Know how to:			
sequence lessons so that knowledge, concepts and skills are introduced in a logical way			
use specific pedagogical approaches in each subject to promote understanding			
develop my subject knowledge			
teach all subjects in the primary national curriculum			

5

MODELLING

━ IN THIS CHAPTER ━

This chapter introduces modelling as a pedagogical approach. We emphasise that modelling makes explicit the subject-specific content and involves processes including demonstrating, questioning, scaffolding and explanations. The chapter introduces the importance of 'thinking aloud' during the modelling process so that teachers can make explicit the thought processes that children also need to consider during their independent learning. The concept of scaffolding is discussed as a key component of modelling. We argue that modelling the process of learning with young children does not just involve the process of demonstration on the whiteboard. We emphasise the importance of combining verbal instructions with visual demonstration so that pupils are not just asked to listen, but they are also required to watch the process of demonstration. This chapter provides useful examples of how to use modelling in all national curriculum subjects.

KEY RESEARCH

Two different types of modelling are described in the literature:

- *Mastery models* demonstrate rapid learning and make no errors. In this type of modelling, the teacher models the task or skill perfectly.

- *Coping models* are not perfect. Teachers show their hesitations and make errors so that they demonstrate approaching the task from the perspective of the pupil.

(Braaksma et al., 2002)

Research has demonstrated that the use of mastery (competent) models is more effective than coping models (Graham and Harris, 1994; Schunk et al., 1987). However, the research is inconclusive. Evidence in other studies suggests that weak learners learn more from focusing their observations on weak models, but better learners learn more from focusing on accurate models. Braaksma et al. (2002) suggest that this is likely to be the case because accurate models are more matched with the cognitive processes of good learners, and weak models are probably more matched with the cognitive processes of weak learners.

Regardless of these research findings, it could be argued that children of all abilities should be introduced to accurate models so that they can aspire to replicate them. There is also value in children observing coping models. Coping models provide an opportunity for teachers to model misconceptions and to model the process of thinking like a learner. This is sometimes referred to as 'thinking aloud', which we address later in the chapter.

KEY POLICY

The early career framework states that teachers should learn that 'modelling helps pupils understand new processes and ideas; accurate models make abstract ideas concrete and accessible' (DfE, 2019a, p15).

WHAT IS MODELLING?

Modelling is the process of making new learning explicit to pupils. It can take a variety of forms. These include:

- demonstrating a process using the body (e.g. demonstrating how to do a forward roll in physical education);

- demonstrating the steps that must be followed to work through a mathematical calculation by writing these out on the whiteboard;

- modelling the process of writing;

- using objects to model a mathematical problem;

- modelling reading with expression;

- demonstrating the skills in art and design or design and technology;

- modelling thought processes (e.g. thinking aloud like a writer);

- demonstrating a scientific investigation;

- modelling sentence structure using 'human sentences';

- demonstrating the process of hot-seating in drama.

These examples illustrate that modelling does not just include demonstrating things on the whiteboard. They also illustrate that modelling involves a great deal more than simply explaining subject content to children. The process involves demonstrating to children the process of learning by making it explicit.

SOCIAL LEARNING THEORY

Bandura (1977) demonstrated through his famous Bobo doll experiment how children replicate the behaviour or processes that they have observed. Modelling is a pedagogical approach that aligns with social learning theory. Social learning, according to Bandura, involves four processes. These are shown below (Figure 5.1).

Figure 5.1

We will now outline these processes in the context of modelling:

- *Attention.* The assumption of social learning theory is that attention is a key element of social learning. In order for children to learn from the modelling process, they must observe what the teacher is doing and saying during the process of modelling.

- *Retention.* Children must then retain the information that they have been exposed to during the modelling process. If retention is poor, then this will impact on how much they learn. Retention can be supported by revisiting content and by retrieval exercises.

- *Reproduction.* Social learning theory assumes that children must have opportunities to practise the learning that they have been exposed to during the modelling process. This will support retention. Examples include practising mathematical calculations or composing writing using structures that they have been taught during the modelling process.

- *Motivation.* Bandura (1977) argued that children need to be motivated in order for learning to take place. Extrinsic motivation can be promoted through the use of praise and tangible rewards, but being intrinsically motivated to complete a task is much more effective.

MODELLING THE STEPS

Breaking subject content down into a series of smaller steps is an effective pedagogical approach. Teachers can provide children with a list of the steps and they can model each step systematically. This approach is particularly effective when teachers provide opportunities for children to practise each step after the step has been modelled. This can be 'guided practice' so that children have an opportunity to gain support either from peers or the teacher before they are expected to work independently. Modelling the steps of a task systematically and providing opportunities for guided practice after each step support children to develop mastery of the subject content. Teachers can use the guided practice phase to identify and address misconceptions that children may have developed before moving on to the next step.

MODELLING ABSTRACT IDEAS

Effective teachers can make abstract content meaningful to children. Abstract subject content may be content that is outside of the child's direct experience. In the example sections later in this chapter, we provide some examples of how to use concrete representations to enable children to understand abstract concepts and ideas. One way of achieving this is to use objects or other visual representations (e.g. diagrams or videos) to make abstract ideas meaningful to children.

SCAFFOLDING

Scaffolding originates from the work of Jerome Bruner. He described it in the following way:

> *[Scaffolding] refers to the steps taken to reduce the degrees of freedom in carrying out some task so that the child can concentrate on the difficult skill she is in the process of acquiring.*

(Bruner, 1978, p19)

It is very similar to Vygotsky's zone of proximal development, which is described as:

> *the distance between the actual developmental level as determined by independent problem solving and the level of potential development as determined through problem-solving under adult guidance, or in collaboration with more capable peers.*

(Vygotsky, 1978, p86)

Vygotsky (1978) emphasised the importance of guidance from adults or more able peers to support children to achieve independent problem-solving. However, Bruner's (1978) concept of scaffolding is helpful because it helps us to understand the role of more capable peers or adults in the process of learning. Both saw learning as a social process – they were social constructivists. Scaffolding as an analogy for learning is a powerful metaphor. When a building is being erected, scaffolding supports the building in a similar way to teachers or more capable peers who support the learning of those who are working at lower stages of development. When the building is strong enough to stay in place without falling down, the scaffolding can be removed. When children have confidently mastered a skill or task under guidance from others, they no longer require the support – they can perform the skill or task independently.

Modelling is a form of scaffolding. The teacher uses modelling to guide the child. Once the child has mastered the subject content, they no longer need the model. They can effectively operate independently. The teacher must strike a fine balance. If they do not provide sufficient modelling, the child may not grasp the subject content. However, if they provide too much modelling, the child may not develop the independence required to complete the task or perform the skill without the model. The aim should be to gradually remove the modelling when it is no longer required in the same way that the scaffolding is removed from a building. If the model is never removed, there is a danger that children will become dependent upon it.

MODELLING METACOGNITIVE STRATEGIES

Metacognition is the process of learning how to learn. It involves the skills of planning, monitoring and evaluating learning so that children achieve the best outcomes. Good learners use these metacognitive strategies all the time, and they are lifelong skills.

Teachers can model metacognitive strategies by modelling how to:

- check the accuracy of mathematical calculations;
- use checklists (success criteria) to monitor the quality of their own work during completion of a task;
- edit work to improve it;
- self-evaluate work against the success criteria;
- use a writing frame to plan a piece of writing.

This is not an exhaustive list, and you should be able to add to it. The key point is that effective learners are strategic learners. They can use the skills of planning, monitoring and evaluating to meet deadlines and goals, as well as improving the quality of their work. Teachers need to explicitly model these strategies because they are not always intuitive.

THINKING ALOUD

Thinking aloud is the process of modelling the thought processes that occur during the completion of a task. It enables teachers to make explicit the thought processes that occur when a learner is approaching a task or performing a skill. It allows teachers to make explicit:

- the steps involved in completing a task or performing a skill;
- the decisions that need to be made during this process;
- checking accuracy, checking for sense and editing work.

QUESTIONING AND EXPLANATIONS

Teachers use questioning not only to check understanding, but also to promote thinking when new subject content is being introduced. In addition, teachers use explanations to help children understand subject content. These are modelling strategies. However, the use of visual cues to support questioning and explanations is particularly helpful during the process of modelling. Explanations can be enhanced with the use of photographs, pictures, diagrams, objects and other resources. Explanations can be enhanced by demonstrating a skill or process. Learning is generally more effective if auditory information is also supported by visual information and other senses, including touch, taste and smell. Using a combination of channels can improve the effectiveness of modelling.

TAKE 5

- Support verbal explanations with diagrams, videos and pictures.

- Model 'thinking aloud' so that the thought processes involved in learning are made explicit to children.

- Model metacognitive strategies in your teaching (e.g. modelling working through a checklist to complete a task or modelling following the steps to complete a mathematical problem).

- Peer-to-peer modelling can be a useful way for more able learners to support children working at lower stages of development.

- Model subject-specific misconceptions as well as producing accurate models.

CLASSROOM EXAMPLE

The visualiser is a very effective piece of equipment for modelling. You can use the visualiser for a variety of purposes. These include:

- producing models of writing;

- sharing accurate models of work and highlighting the features that make the work good;

- recording children's ideas to produce a written record;

- modelling how to mark a piece of work;

- placing objects on the visualiser in order to display them on the screen.

WHAT DOES GOOD PRACTICE IN MODELLING LOOK LIKE IN THE CLASSROOM?

This section provides examples of how modelling can be used in different national curriculum subjects in the primary school.

MODELLING IN ENGLISH

In English, the teacher models the process of writing. They model the structural and language features of different text types, and during this process they use the 'thinking aloud' strategy. They might start a piece of writing on the whiteboard, but during this process they model the decisions that a writer needs to make by articulating their thought processes. They use a running commentary as they model the writing, which is verbalised to the children. They might say things such as:

- 'How shall I start this off?'

- 'I need to use a better word here.'

- 'Let me check this to see if it makes sense.'

- 'I want to include some dialogue to make it more interesting for the reader.'

- 'I need to use an adjective to give the reader more information here.'

In handwriting, the teacher models correct letter formation. The teacher reminds the children where to position the pencil to start the letter. The teacher then models the direction that the pencil needs to move in to form the letter correctly. The teacher then models how to finish the letter. The teacher demonstrates how to produce ascenders and descenders. The teacher then repeats the model again with the same letter, but this time the teacher asks the pupils to participate by tracing the letter in the air as the teacher writes it on the whiteboard. The teacher then repeats the process again by asking the children to trace the letter on the palms of their hands as the teacher writes it on the whiteboard. The teacher then gives them small whiteboards and asks them to observe the teacher modelling the letter formation before asking them to practise the formation on their whiteboards. The teacher observes them closely as they are working to check that they are starting and forming the letters in the correct places. This activity is best completed in small groups so that the teacher can monitor the accuracy of letter formation easily.

MODELLING IN MATHEMATICS

The teacher models the steps through a mathematical problem. They display the steps on the whiteboard and they systematically model each step. They then provide children with an opportunity for some guided practice, perhaps by providing the class with a similar question to complete in pairs, which they provide feedback on. When they are sure that children have understood, they provide a task for them to complete independently.

The teacher models the concept of 'difference' by using towers of cubes. First, the teacher constructs a tower of ten cubes. The teacher counts them with the children. Then the teacher constructs a tower of six cubes. Again, they count them. The teacher stands the two towers next to each other and asks, 'What is the difference between six and ten?' The teacher models how to answer this question by counting the four cubes that make one tower taller than the other.

The teacher models the process of using a number line to count on for addition. She writes '5 + 13' on the whiteboard. She models starting at 13 (the largest number first). She then emphasises the importance of not counting the starting number. She then models counting on 5 more by doing five jumps on the number line. She explains that the last number (18) is the answer. She then gives the children a different calculation and asks them to tell her the steps through the problem. They guide her by explaining what number to start on and how many jumps to do, and they check that she has landed on the correct number. She repeats this another time, but this time she makes a deliberate mistake in the modelling process to identify if the children notice this. She then provides each child with a number line and gives them a calculation to solve on their own. She asks them for the answer and then models the process again on the whiteboard.

MODELLING IN SCIENCE

The teacher models a scientific investigation by demonstrating it to the class. They demonstrate how to construct an electrical circuit. They model several times how to do this incorrectly and use this as an opportunity to discuss with the class why the bulb does not light. They then use correct modelling to make the bulb light. The children then work in pairs to construct their own circuits.

MODELLING IN HISTORY

The teacher uses a range of Victorian artefacts (primary sources) to explain to children what life was like in the past and how it was different to life today. Explanations are enhanced by objects. The teacher has Victorian objects and modern-day equivalent objects so that children can see how things have changed. The teacher then extends the children's thinking by asking them to consider why the Victorian iron does not have an electric cable or plug.

MODELLING IN GEOGRAPHY

The teacher models the process of constructing a map of the classroom using a simple key. The children are involved in making decisions about how to represent classroom objects on the key.

MODELLING IN ART AND DESIGN

The teacher models the skill of colour mixing using dry powder paints, including the process of dipping the brush in water, selecting one colour and adding the colour to the mixing palette. There is then modelling of the process of cleaning the brush in water before selecting a different colour and mixing this in the palette with the first colour. This process is used to model changing primary colours into secondary colours.

MODELLING IN DESIGN AND TECHNOLOGY

The teacher models the skill of how to safely saw two pieces of wood using a bench hook. The teacher then demonstrates how to join the two pieces of wood by creating a joint with cardboard triangles and glue. The children are then required to practise this skill, and in subsequent lessons they are asked to use this skill to make a wooden vehicle that will travel.

The teacher demonstrates how to create a running stitch using fabric with holes in, a needle and some wool. How to thread the needle and then tie a knot in the end of the wool is also demonstrated. The teacher models slowly how to create the stitch. After demonstrating a few stitches, the teacher then asks the children to say what to do next. The teacher models creating a line of stitches and then demonstrates to the children how to start a new line.

MODELLING IN PHYSICAL EDUCATION

The teacher demonstrates the process of doing a forward roll. The teacher uses live commentary to make pertinent teaching points so that children perform this skill safely. The teacher says:

- 'This is my starting position.'

- 'This is where I place my hands.'

- 'I must not let my head touch the ground because this is dangerous.'

- 'I must use my arms to push me over.'

MODELLING IN MUSIC

The teacher models pitch. The teacher plays a musical instrument using a high and low pitch. The teacher then repeats this with different instruments and asks the children to identify whether the pitch is high or low.

MODELLING IN COMPUTING

The teacher demonstrates to the children how to use a specific piece of software. Modelling is used to demonstrate all the different features of the software so that the children understand how to use the it. The children are then given an opportunity to use the software independently.

CHAPTER CHECKLIST

	Accessed	Secure	Confident
Know that:			
modelling involves a variety of pedagogical approaches			
Know how to:			
use explanations to promote understanding			
use demonstrations to promote understanding			
articulate the thinking process out loud during modelling			
model metacognitive strategies			
use modelling in all primary national curriculum subjects			

6

INCLUSION

— IN THIS CHAPTER —

This chapter introduces you to key research on inclusive education. It emphasises the need to differentiate appropriately for all children and the importance of understanding the factors that inhibit pupil learning. Throughout the chapter, practical guidance is offered to support you to overcome these, and the implications of legislation and policy are outlined. The chapter argues that many children with special educational needs and disabilities will benefit from pre-teaching, and some examples of effective practice are provided to support you in the classroom. Additionally, it is essential that teaching assistants are deployed effectively. Existing research is highlighted in order to illuminate examples of effective and impactful deployment, as well as supporting you to avoid common pitfalls.

KEY RESEARCH

Research suggests that inclusive education increases social and academic opportunities for both children with and without disabilities, as well as significantly increasing life outcomes for children with disabilities (Florian et al., 2017; Hehir et al., 2016).

KEY POLICY

The teachers' standards state that teachers must:

- know when and how to differentiate appropriately, using approaches that enable pupils to be taught effectively;

- have a secure understanding of how a range of factors can inhibit pupils' ability to learn, and how best to overcome these;

- demonstrate an awareness of the physical, social and intellectual development of children, and know how to adapt teaching to support pupils' education at different stages of development;

- have a clear understanding of the needs of all pupils, including those with special educational needs, those of high ability, those with English as an additional language and those with disabilities, as well as being able to use and evaluate distinctive teaching approaches to engage and support them.

(DfE, 2011)

In addition, all primary schools must meet their legal duties in relation to the Equality Act 2010 (HM Government, 2010). This places a legal duty on schools to protect children with protected characteristics from direct or indirect discrimination, and to promote good relations between children with protected characteristics and those without. The legislation requires schools to provide reasonable adjustments to address the needs of children with disabilities. There are nine protected characteristics, but the ones that apply to children in primary school include:

- disability;

- gender reassignment;

- race, religion or belief;

- sex;

- sexual orientation.

The code of practice for special educational needs and disabilities is a key policy framework that all schools must address (DfE and DoH, 2015). The code of practice identifies the responsibilities of teachers, school leaders and local authorities in relation to meeting children's needs. It emphasises the need for schools to work in partnership with pupils, parents and external agencies to address children's needs. It identifies four categories of needs. These include communication and language needs, cognition and learning needs, social, emotional and mental health needs, and sensory and physical needs. The code includes a clear definition of special educational needs and disabilities.

WHAT IS INCLUSION?

Inclusion places an onus upon schools to examine the environmental, curricular and pedagogical factors that limit achievement (Erten and Savage, 2012), resulting in radical reform of pedagogy and value systems (Mittler, 2000). Inclusion necessitates proactive responses from schools to meet the needs of all learners (Farrell, 2001; Mittler, 2000; Nind, 2005). It requires schools to adapt their policies and practices to meet the needs of all learners rather than the child adapting to fit in with the school. Inclusion emphasises the rights of all pupils to participate and achieve in education. It is fundamentally about equality of opportunity by removing barriers to participation, learning and achievement.

According to the United Nations, inclusive education means:

- a fundamental right to education;

- a principle that values students' well-being, dignity, autonomy and contribution to society;

- a continuing process to eliminate barriers to education and promote reform in the culture, policy and practice in schools to include all students.

(UN, 2016)

Some academics have emphasised that all children have a right to be in the same educational space (Cobley, 2018; Florian et al., 2017; Hehir et al., 2016; Schuelka and Johnstone, 2012), although this association between location and inclusion is often contested. The assumption that special schools and special units within mainstream schools cannot be inclusive can be challenged based on the quality of the education that children receive. It could be argued that the association between inclusion and the location in which schooling takes place emphasises the process of assimilation rather than the quality of the child's experience and their learning.

Avramidis et al. (2002) have noted that inclusion 'is a bewildering concept which can have a variety of interpretations and applications' (p158). As such, it has become an elusive and empty term (Gabel, 2010), and consequently Cole (2005) makes a useful point in arguing that it is better to explore *meanings* rather than *the meaning* of inclusion. The vested interests of politicians, teachers, parents and people with disabilities will invariably shape their personal perspectives of inclusion. However, the development of socially just pedagogies continually evolves through being grounded in personal experience (Sikes et al., 2007).

Inclusion has been reflected metaphorically in the literature as a journey (Ainscow, 2000; Allan, 2000; Azzopardi, 2010; Nind, 2005). Julie Allan's humorous reference to the term 'inconclusive education' (Allan, 2000, p43) serves as a reminder that inclusion is always in process and never complete. In this respect, inclusion challenges schools and teachers to continually develop their capacities to reach out to all learners (Ainscow, 2000) by developing socially just pedagogies that connect individual learners with their own ways of learning (Corbett, 2001). Inclusion necessitates a deep cultural change within schools (Corbett, 1999; Graham and Harwood, 2011) to make schools more able to respond to difference. It places an onus upon schools to examine the environmental, curricular and pedagogical factors that limit achievement (Erten and Savage, 2012), resulting in radical reform of pedagogy and value systems (Mittler, 2000). Such an approach represents an ecological perspective (Dyson et al., 2004) that challenges educators to examine factors in the school environment which limit achievement rather than focusing on deficits within individual learners.

Azzopardi (2009, 2010) has argued that the term 'inclusive education' is little more than a cliché: 'a politically correct term that is used for speeches and policy-makers to silence all woes' (Azzopardi, 2009, p21). It is defined in various ways by different groups with different interests, leading to its exploitation (Sikes et al., 2007). For example, Hodkinson and Vickerman (2009) have argued that government definitions of inclusion have continued to emphasise the traditional discourses of special educational needs. In addition, inclusion is interpreted differently within and across various groups (Glazzard, 2011).

During the past three decades, inclusion has become a politically correct term (Azzopardi, 2010) for politicians, theorists and activists, and this has diverted attention away from its realisation in practice. Pather (2007) argues that there is a need to 'de-sloganise' inclusion by focusing on providing quality experiences for all learners. However, inclusion is political because it demands, and continues to require, a structural transformation of the structures that underpin the education system to make education more equitable and more responsive to diversity. It has been argued that until inclusion is disentangled from neoliberal values, teachers will be restricted in the extent to which they are able to develop socially just pedagogies (Slee, 2011). This restricts inclusion to a process of assimilation, thus resembling the previous discourses of *integration* in which schools accommodated learners with special educational needs but their systems were largely unchanged.

Like others (Slee, 2001a, 2001b, 2011; Slee and Allan, 2001; Thomas and Loxley, 2007), we argue that the special educational needs paradigm that has dominated education for the last three decades is exclusionary and serves the function of maintaining existing inequalities. Questions of inclusion should concern questions of *rights* rather than *needs* (Roaf, 1988). Needs are problematic because a need implies a deficit in relation to a socially constructed norm. In England, it has been argued that educational policies have allowed inclusive education to be used as a replacement for special needs education (Black-Hawkins et al., 2007; Slee, 2011). Consequently, rather than inclusion interrogating and reconstructing the existing structures, policies and practices of schooling and challenging deeply ingrained injustices, it has sustained inequalities by creating subtle forms of segregation (Slee, 2011). It could therefore be argued that through its connection with special needs, inclusion – as a policy discourse – has served to protect the status quo in schools (Graham and Slee, 2008; Slee, 2011). As a concept, inclusion has continued to focus on notions of *assimilation* and *presence* rather than representing a struggle for equality and social justice (Hodkinson, 2012). The continued dominance of the use of traditional psychological approaches for responding to diversity has resulted in categorisation, stigmatisation and deficit views of difference that have not helped the inclusion agenda (Florian, 2009). Researchers have argued that inclusion must be disassociated from special educational needs so that it is able, as a policy discourse, to articulate its distinct values (Slee, 2011) based on social justice, democracy and equity. It necessitates a departure from existing processes that label, segregate and stigmatise to enable schools to embrace diversity (Graham and Harwood, 2011).

Cole's (2005) narratives of women teachers are helpful in exploring interpretations of inclusion. They explore the collective voices of six women who were both mothers and teachers of children with special educational needs and disabilities. Within the narratives, the mother-teachers emphasised the need for educators to embrace humanitarian values (Armstrong, 2005) by developing a pedagogy that emphasises care, dignity and respect. The emphasis on 'careful teaching' is also prominent in the early writings of Jenny Corbett (e.g. Corbett, 1992). The experience of becoming parents had a substantially positive impact on the professional identities of these teachers (Cole, 2005), and this theme has been identified in previous research (Sikes, 1997). The mother-teachers embraced the language of 'normality' by viewing difference as *normal* rather than *special*. In doing so, they rejected the deficit, pathologising language of special educational needs. Thus, inclusion necessitates a humanitarian approach to teaching that emphasises care, respect and dignity. In addition, inclusion requires creative and reflective educators who are willing to experiment with pedagogy (Allan, 2006) and who view diversity as an 'enriching opportunity for learning' (Pizzuto, 2010, p88).

Lloyd's (2008) call for a reconceptualisation of achievement and the 'denormalisation of institutions, systems and rules which comprise education and schooling' (p228) is a critical argument. Such a transformation demands major changes to the education system (Nilholm, 2006) through disrupting the current structures of schooling that result in segregation and systemic failure. Inclusion raises critical questions about the purposes of education and challenges politicians to reconceptualise current limited notions of achievement. Transforming pedagogical approaches is insufficient to facilitate social justice. In order to develop inclusive schools, the existing structures of schooling (i.e. the curriculum and assessment processes) need to be transformed to enable education to respond to diversity. However, changing schools and school systems is problematic because no perfect alternatives exist (Nind et al., 2003), and a variety of models and approaches to inclusion, rather than 'one size fits all', will be required. The notion of inclusion as a transformation of educational policies and practices is a well-established theme within the literature (Farrell, 2001; Mittler, 2000; Nind, 2005).

Philosophical debates have emphasised that hopes for full inclusion are fundamentally naive because schools and communities will always need to employ exclusionary strategies in order to secure their own existence (Hansen, 2012; Wilson, 1999, 2000). The thrust of such critiques is that in practice, inclusion always has limits. Hegarty (2001) warned that inclusion would have a case to answer if it diverted attention away from a school's core function of promoting learning towards a focus of promoting values of equity and social justice. While these critiques are conceptually sound, they do not sufficiently articulate how the current structures of schooling (curricula, assessment processes, limited notions of what constitutes achievement) create barriers to participation and achievement that subsequently result in exclusion. Inclusion is crucially about the politics of difference and identity (Slee, 2001b), which critically interrogates the existing structures, policies and practices of schooling (Slee, 2011).

Inclusion demands a process of educational reconstruction and revisioning (Slee, 2001a) rather than a process of assimilation into an unchanged system. Such limited notions of inclusion, which have been uncritically accepted, will inevitably result in exclusion, and consequently inclusion will always fail as a policy imperative (Slee, 2011). It could be argued that educators should not dismiss inclusion because it takes time to get it right or because they make inevitable mistakes along the way (Cole, 2005). Instead, they might consider using inclusion as a vehicle for experimenting with creative, innovative approaches in a bid to reach out to all learners (Allan, 2006; Goodley and Runswick-Cole, 2010).

THE PROBLEM WITH 'NEEDS'

The concept of 'need' is highly problematic in that it reinforces notions of *deficit* and *disadvantage* (Thomas and Loxley, 2007). Additionally, within the discourses of special education, 'need' and notions of 'normality' are determined through distances from artificially constructed norms (Graham, 2006). Failure to achieve such norms results in the creation of an othered group made up of learners who do not fit the required subject construction – able, productive, skilled learners who understand their responsibilities to a neoliberal, marketised society (Goodley, 2007). These learners are reconceptualised as the needs of the school (to compete, to maintain standards and order) are transferred to the learner (Thomas and Loxley, 2007), thus inscribing a stigmatised identity. They are by-products of a traditional curriculum (Skrtic, 1991) in which they are viewed as eternally lacking (Goodley, 2007), and with support they are expected to transform themselves to meet the required subject construction. The diagnosis, intervention and remediation processes result in 'the entrapment of the child in a cocoon of professional help' (Thomas and Loxley, 2007, p55), which conceals the vested professional interests of 'expert' professionals under the rhetoric of humanitarianism (Tomlinson, 1985). These learners are then singled out for specialist attention and placed under increased surveillance (Allan, 1996), resulting in them becoming disempowered.

The vocabulary of individual intervention, targets and individual education plans advocated in the code of practice results in a 'highly individualised approach' (Skidmore, 2004, p15) that locates the deficiencies within the child rather than the deficiencies within the school (Dyson, 2001). Such approaches restrict creative pedagogy (Skidmore, 2004) and, according to Lloyd (2008), are 'all concerned with normalization and ... standardization, of groups and individuals rather than contributing to the denormalization of the institutions' (p228), which is so central to the development of inclusion. Inclusion is a transformative process that refutes 'normative practices' (Graham, 2006, p7) such as diagnoses and the use of 'correct training' (Foucault, 1975, 1977, 1984). These serve as disciplinary forces that regulate the lives of individuals (Armstrong, 2005). Normative practices are deeply embedded in the discourses of special educational needs and, while failing to promote equity, serve to legitimise failure by emphasising 'individual responsibility for individual achievement'

(Armstrong, 2005, p147). Such practices, which serve to negate diversity, are justified because they are viewed as benevolent responses to need (Graham, 2006).

It has been argued that special needs educators have relocated their knowledge and experiences within the discourses of inclusion. Consequently, this has restricted inclusion and enabled the medical model of disability to triumph (Slee, 2001b). This model is discussed in the following section. Varying 'disorders' have been introduced into the lexicon of special needs, each with its own symptoms and disease-like characteristics, creating spectacle, fear and revulsion (Dunne, 2009). Intervention and remediation serve to negate diversity by creating normative subjects, and educators have been positioned as 'police' (Dunne, 2009), charged with hunting down abnormalities and correcting them through early identification processes. In contrast, an inclusive pedagogy rejects both deficit views of difference and fixed notions of intelligence (Florian, 2009), which are heavily embedded within the discourses of special educational needs.

MODELS OF DISABILITY

In this section, three models of disability are discussed: the medical model, the social model and the affirmative model.

MEDICAL MODEL

The psycho-medical model of disability 'conceptualizes difficulties in learning as arising from deficits in the neurological or psychological make-up of the child' (Skidmore, 2004, p2). Until the 1980s, it was the dominant model that influenced the way people thought about disability. The model views disability as a biological construct, located within a person, which needs to be treated in order to cure the person. The model influenced the language of disability through terminology such as 'syndrome', 'symptoms' and 'disorder'; terms that are still used in contemporary society. Thomas and Loxley (2007) argue that biological perspectives on impairment and disability place insufficient emphasis on the wider environment in which learning occurs.

We have represented this model using the diagram in Figure 6.1.

The model essentially positions the individual as a tragic person, with disability viewed as a tragedy. The medical model assumes that biological impairments are the cause of disablement. The assumption of the model is that the disability needs to be diagnosed (through assessment) and then it needs to be named (labelling). The model assumes that once the disability has been diagnosed, it then needs to be 'treated' and cured. External specialists play a role in assessing and diagnosing the disability. These may include doctors, educational psychologists or professionals from other professions.

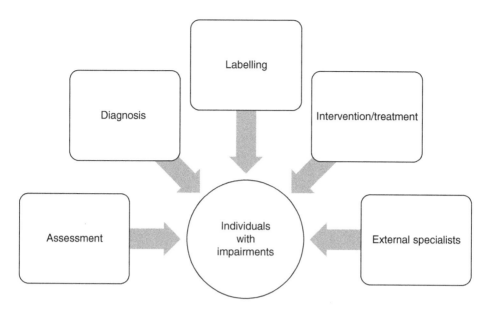

Figure 6.1

SOCIAL MODEL

The growth of disability activism in the 1980s led to the development of the social model of disability (Barnes, 1991; Oliver, 1990). Unlike the medical model, the social model locates the problem of disability squarely within society (Oliver, 1996). The model assumes that disability 'is an artificial and exclusionary social construction that penalises those people with impairments who do not conform to mainstream expectations of appearance, behaviour and/or economic performance' (Tregaskis, 2002, p457).

Crucially, the model separates *impairment* from *disability*. Impairment is a biological construct within a person. However, the fundamental principle of the social model is that impairment does not need to become disabling. Disability is defined in terms of access to goods and services.

The assumption of the social model is that with the correct societal adaptations, people with impairments are still able to access goods and services such as education, housing and employment. Adaptations can be physical (such as lifts or ramps), attitudinal or financial, but are not restricted to these categories.

It has been argued that the social model has been an emancipatory force in the lives of many people with disabilities (Tregaskis, 2002), although critical literature has emphasised how the social model can sometimes underplay the severity of some impairments and the way in which these may prevent access to goods and services (Dewsbury et al., 2004).

Despite this critique, the social model shifts the discourse from one of 'needs' (as in the medical model) to a discourse that emphasises 'rights'. Roaf and Bines (1989) argued that a focus on 'needs' detracts from an emphasis on 'rights', which the social model privileges.

We have represented the affirmative model in the following diagram (Figure 6.2).

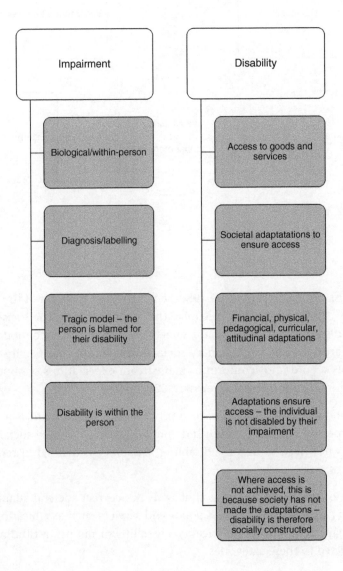

Figure 6.2

AFFIRMATIVE MODEL

The principles of the social model were extended by Swain and French with the development of the affirmative model. The affirmative model:

is essentially a non-tragic view of disability and impairment which encompasses positive social identities, both individual and collective, for disabled people grounded in the benefits of lifestyle and life experiences of being impaired and disabled.

(Swain and French, 2003, p150)

While the model recognises disability as a social construction, it calls for a positive affirmation of disability so that people with disabilities are able to reclaim their disabled identities by proudly owning their disability and celebrating it. The model resists the use of 'within-person' interventions that seek to eradicate disability from people's lives. It views disability as a positive and energising force that brings diversity into the world.

We have represented the model as follows (Figure 6.3).

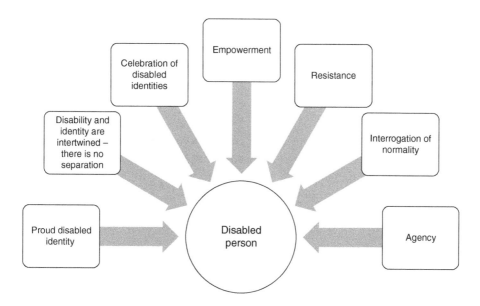

Figure 6.3

The affirmative model provides validation for the disabled identity. It does not view the disabled identity as inferior to non-disabled identities. Disability is viewed as a positive identity, and the disabled person can 'claim' their identity and be proud of it. It is who they are. They are not a person with a disability because this separates them from their disability. Their disabled identity is a fundamental aspect of their identity and they are proud of it. The model therefore empowers them to reclaim their disabled identity but also provides empowerment because their disability is validated, and therefore they are recognised as having equal status to non-disabled individuals. The model incorporates resistance because it is a 'pushback' against the non-disabled majority who historically have been positioned as superior to the minority with disabilities. The model therefore critically interrogates the concept of 'normality' and assumes that diversity is a positive and energising force which makes the world a better place. The model assigns agency to disabled people because it assumes that they have a right to lead productive and fulfilling lives by engaging in education and employment, as well as participating in personal and sexual relationships.

BIOPSYCHOSOCIAL MODEL OF HEALTH

Rather than viewing the models as distinct and oppositional, it could be argued that the models could be mutually supportive. The World Health Organization released the biopsychosocial model of health, the International Classification of Functioning, Disability and Health (ICF) (WHO, 2001), which aims to provide a holistic definition of health by essentially merging the medical and social models. The model recognises the complex interrelationships between biological and contextual factors that influence how disability is experienced by the individual. These are identified below:

- *Body functions and structures.* The body functions and structures of people: problems with the integrity of structures or their functions are termed 'impairments' (functioning at the level of the body).

- *Activity.* The activities/tasks people undertake: difficulties undertaking those are termed 'activity limitations' (functioning at the level of the individual).

- *Participation.* The participation/involvement of people in life situations: difficulties are termed 'participation restrictions' (functioning of a person as a member of society).

- *Environmental factors.* The external factors (physical, social and attitudinal) that affect people's experiences (and whether these factors are facilitators or barriers).

- *Personal factors.* These are the internal factors that affect people's experiences (and whether these factors are facilitators or barriers).

(WHO, 2001)

The ICF was created to define/describe health but recognises that a breakdown/problem with any of the components can affect health experiences. For instance, an impairment of a body function may exist, but the impact of that is only seen when we consider how it affects an individual's ability to perform a task or participate in a life situation, and the degree to which that participation is affected is moderated by contextual factors (personal and environmental) that act as barriers/facilitators.

The model is represented as follows (Figure 6.4).

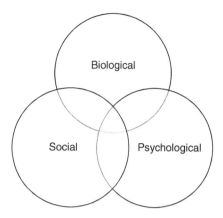

Figure 6.4

Biological factors include the child's physical health, disability or genetic structures. Social factors include family circumstances, peer influences and school interactions. Psychological factors include resilience, self-esteem and motivation.

The model demonstrates the complex interrelationship between the biological, social and psychological factors that influence health.

The model demonstrates how mental health can be influenced by all of these factors, as well as how factors overlap. For example, adverse circumstances in the family (social factors) can influence the child's physical health (biological factors) and their mental health (psychological factors).

Often the models of disability are represented as though they are distinct, and the critical literature on the medical model (Thomas and Loxley, 2007) underplays the role that a person's biological impairments can play in restricting access to goods and services. However, the implementation of interventions that address biological and contextual factors can potentially have a greater impact than operating within the principles of one model in isolation to the others.

TRAINING FOR TEACHERS

Traditionally, training in inclusive education strategies was offered as continuing professional development and one-off workshops. However, there is increasing evidence that one-off training events do not impact significantly on pedagogical and structural changes in schools (Fullan, 2007; Kuroda et al., 2017; Rose and Doveston, 2015). It is more effective to embed inclusive pedagogy into initial teacher education programmes for trainee teachers, as well as providing sustained and continuous in-service professional development for qualified teachers. These approaches positively shape teachers' attitudes towards inclusion by emphasising the responsibilities of teachers rather than specialists for meeting the needs of all children (Forlin and Chambers, 2011; Graham and Scott, 2016; Sharma et al., 2015; Subban and Mahlo, 2017).

QUALITY-FIRST TEACHING

Evidence from research strongly suggests that inclusive teaching practices raise the achievement of all children in the classroom (Sailor, 2015), not just the achievement of learners with special educational needs and disabilities. Thus, inclusive teaching is synonymous with high-quality teaching. Learners with special educational needs and disabilities do not necessarily require different activities and different pedagogical approaches. They require access to high-quality inclusive teaching that meets the needs of all learners.

SCHOOL LEADERSHIP

Evidence suggests that the school leadership team is crucial for the successful implementation of inclusive education (Shogren et al., 2015; Villa and Thousand, 2016). School leadership teams have a responsibility to ensure that:

- everyone is made to feel welcome;
- students are equally valued;
- there are high expectations for all students;
- staff and students treat one another with respect;
- there is a partnership between staff and families;
- the school is accessible to all students;
- senior staff support teachers in making sure that all students participate and learn;
- the school monitors the presence, participation and achievement of all students.

(IBE-UNESCO, 2016)

CURRICULAR FLEXIBILITY AND LEARNING OUTCOMES

Research strongly suggests that an increase in the diversity and breadth of learning outcomes, coupled with an increase in the breadth of the curriculum, facilitates the successful implementation of inclusive education (Nelson, 2014; Sæbønes et al., 2015). Some research also suggests that personalised learning for individual students can be very successful (Carpenter et al., 2017; Rhim and Lancet, 2018).

PRE-TEACHING

Many children with special educational needs and disabilities will benefit from pre-teaching. Pre-teaching provides an opportunity for you to teach the knowledge, concepts and skills that you will cover subsequently in the lesson. This ensures that these children are not placed at a disadvantage during the lesson because they might take longer to process the subject content. Pre-teaching can be used to develop familiarity with key texts, vocabulary, concepts, knowledge and skills prior to the lesson so that children with special educational needs and disabilities can participate more effectively during the lesson (Trundley et al., 2017).

CONSOLIDATION AND PRACTICE

Many children benefit from opportunities to consolidate their knowledge, understanding and skills before moving on to the next stage in learning (Hattie and Donoghue, 2016). This does not just apply to children with special educational needs. When you plan sequences of lessons, consider building in opportunities to recap on subject content that has already been taught. Always recap on prior learning at the start of lessons. Before moving on to something new, provide children with opportunities to apply their understanding of subject content in different contexts to ensure that they are developing higher-level thinking and independence skills. It is important for teaching assistants to encourage children to complete tasks independently rather than fostering a culture of dependency. It is also important for teaching assistants to have high expectations of all children.

EFFECTIVE DEPLOYMENT OF TEACHING ASSISTANTS

In 2015, the Education Endowment Foundation (EEF) published its report on the deployment of teaching assistants (TAs). The report was provided in order to offer practical and evidence-based guidance to help primary and secondary schools make the best use of teaching assistants. Within the report, there are seven key recommendations. These are:

- TAs should not be used as an informal teaching resource for low-attaining pupils.

- Use TAs to add value to what teachers do, not replace them.

- Use TAs to help pupils develop independent learning skills and manage their own learning.

- Ensure TAs are fully prepared for their role in the classroom.

- Use TAs to deliver high-quality one-to-one and small group support using structured interventions.

- Adopt evidence-based interventions to support TAs in their small group and one-to-one instruction.

- Ensure explicit connections are made between learning from everyday classroom teaching structured interventions.

(EEF, 2015)

This research found that children with the highest level of need were often placed with TAs, which restricted their exposure to qualified teachers. This study found that the children who were most supported by TAs were those with special educational needs and disabilities, and consequently these children made less progress than those who spent most of their time with a teacher (EEF, 2015). In addition, typical deployment arrangements led to a dependency effect, and TAs tended to focus on task completion rather than promoting learning (EEF, 2015). The research reported that in cases where structured interventions were delivered by qualified teachers, the children made greater progress (EEF, 2015).

MEETING THE NEEDS OF VERY ABLE PUPILS

Some children in your class will require tasks that require additional cognitive demand. They may be 'outriders' in that they may be working at a level above anyone else in the class in specific subjects. It does not follow that they will demonstrate this same level of ability across all subjects. These pupils still need to feel part of a group and part of a classroom. They should not be separated from others to work individually because this fosters a sense of exclusion. You might need to provide them with a different task, but it is good practice to still have them seated at a table with other pupils. Strategies for challenging these pupils include:

- including specific questions in your lessons that you directly ask these children to respond to;

- setting a task that focuses on the same content as the rest of the class but promotes a higher level of thinking (e.g. some children need to focus on the application of knowledge to extend their learning, but others may be focusing on understanding knowledge, which is a lower level of thinking);

- setting an open-ended problem-solving task that has multiple solutions;

- expecting greater productivity and quality of work (e.g. in writing tasks);

- developing mastery in a specific learning objective by applying the learning to different contexts;

- working on a learning objective from a higher-level year group, provided that prior learning has been mastered.

(Bobis et al., 2012; Florian and Beaton, 2018)

PUPILS WITH ENGLISH AS AN ADDITIONAL LANGUAGE

Children with English as an additional language do not necessarily have special educational needs. Their difficulties in learning may arise because they are in the process of learning another language rather than due to an underlying difficulty. They will benefit from being immersed in a social and communication-rich environment. They may benefit from a structured language and communication intervention. Pre-teaching vocabulary and texts is a useful strategy to maximise their participation during lessons. Aim to support your explanations and modelling with visual cues, manipulatives and other resources. Provide concrete manipulative resources to support their learning and allow them to code-switch between English and their first language if they cannot identify the word in English.

Cummins' (1980) model of bilingualism demonstrates that children will draw upon understandings from their first language in order to support them to learn an additional language. This existing understanding acts as an 'anchor' to further learning of and through additional languages (Bligh, 2014). Cummins (1980) refers to this as common underlying proficiency (CUP), which includes basic interpersonal communication skills (BICS) and cognitive academic language proficiency (CALP).

BICS refers to social and conversational language and the surface skills of listening and speaking, including observing non-verbal behaviours and reactions, voice cues, and imagery. These are often learned through playful social participation with speakers of the same language (Bligh, 2014). On the other hand, CALP relates specifically to the language of the academic classroom, where non-verbal cues are typically absent and literacy demands are much higher. This therefore includes the necessary knowledge and skills required to work academically in a classroom, as well as the ability to think in and use language as a tool for learning (Figure 6.5).

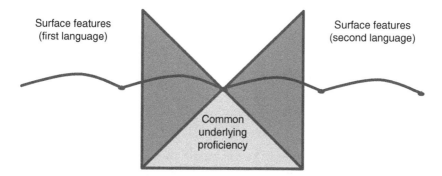

Figure 6.5

The model is represented by two icebergs that are separated above the surface of the water. The peak of each iceberg represents a language, and despite appearing visibly different they merge into one below the surface. It is CUP, which is found below the surface, that enables bilingual learners to function in more than one language. However, if a child is lacking CUP in one language, then it is likely that they will find it difficult to learn another.

It is therefore clear that language and communication interventions in a second language will be ineffective if a child has not met the required threshold of CUP in their first language. This has clear implications in relation to the content and structure of intervention programmes. It demonstrates that interventions must be appropriate and responsive to the needs of individual children in relation to the explicit and meaningful development of BICS and CALP. For example, offering children the opportunity to practise verbal conversations is not cognitively demanding, and as such will support the development of BICS. This is because this activity allows children to practise conversational language and listening and speaking skills. On the other hand, scientific investigations will be cognitively demanding and promote the development of CALP. This is because scientific investigations will expose children to subject-specific vocabulary and the knowledge and skills required to work and think academically.

TAKE 5

- Pre-teach knowledge, concepts and skills to support children with special educational needs and disabilities.

- Provide explicit opportunities for children to consolidate their knowledge, understanding and skills.

- Use teaching assistants to support teachers to deliver structured interventions rather than to replace them.

- Plan activities that expose all children to the same content and provide opportunities for higher-level thinking.

- Plan language and communication interventions that are responsive to children's existing proficiencies in their first language.

CLASSROOM EXAMPLE

When you begin to teach a new class, you should talk to colleagues and specialist practitioners and collect any assessment information relating to the performance of each child. Using this, create profiles detailing age, gender and language proficiency, as well as notes about any specific observations in relation to each child's learning needs. You can add information about interests and motivations once you begin to develop relationships. These profiles should be used to help you tailor your teaching to each child's needs and plan for any modifications that may be required in your teaching and planning.

WHAT DOES GOOD PRACTICE IN INCLUSION LOOK LIKE IN THE CLASSROOM?

Quality-first teaching ensures that planning and implementation are designed and delivered to meet the needs of all children. This approach requires you to have high expectations of all children, including those with special educational needs. Quality-first teaching therefore includes your daily interactions with children and the approaches and strategies that you use to motivate and engage them. When children require further support, in addition to your quality-first teaching, it is appropriate to offer additional interventions to enable children to make the progress that they are expected to. An additional layer of intervention can then be used to support these approaches by offering highly personalised interventions. This three-wave model prioritises inclusive teaching, and therefore promotes good teaching and learning for all. It ensures that children have access to quality-first teaching, as well as additional and personalised interventions for those that require them.

CHAPTER CHECKLIST

	Accessed	Secure	Confident
Know that:			
the code of practice is a legal framework and I understand its principles and the four areas of needs			
Know how to:			
identify special educational needs			
plan adaptations to support children with special educational needs			
plan adaptations to support children with English as an additional language			
plan adaptations to support more able children			

7
ASSESSMENT FOR LEARNING

━━ **IN THIS CHAPTER** ━━

This chapter introduces you to key research on assessment for learning. It emphasises the importance of assessment for learning in raising standards of achievement, and a range of strategies are outlined to support you to integrate assessment tasks within your lessons. The chapter offers practical guidance in relation to questioning, as well as explaining the role of assessment in relation to identifying and addressing misconceptions. The chapter argues that it is not necessary to mark every single piece of work in detail or to mark every child's exercise book, and approaches to marking and feedback are discussed to reduce your workload while maintaining the quality of the feedback that you offer. Effective practice is illustrated through case studies.

KEY RESEARCH

There is consistent evidence that assessment for learning increases pupils' achievement (Hayward and Spencer, 2010; Webb and Jones, 2009). The work of Black and Wiliam (1998) has also been influential in highlighting the benefits of assessment for learning:

> *There is a body of firm evidence that formative assessment is an essential component of classroom work and that its development can raise standards of achievement. We know of no other way of raising standards for which such a strong prima facie case can be made.*

(p12)

KEY POLICY

The teachers' standards state that teachers must:

- know and understand how to assess the relevant subject and curriculum areas, including statutory assessment requirements;

- make use of evidence from formative and summative assessment to secure pupils' progress by adapting planning and teaching;

- give pupils regular feedback, both orally and through accurate marking, and encourage pupils to respond to the feedback.

(DfE, 2011)

In addition, the education inspection framework (Ofsted, 2019) states that 'teachers and leaders use assessment well, for example to help learners embed and use knowledge fluently or to check understanding and inform teaching' (p10).

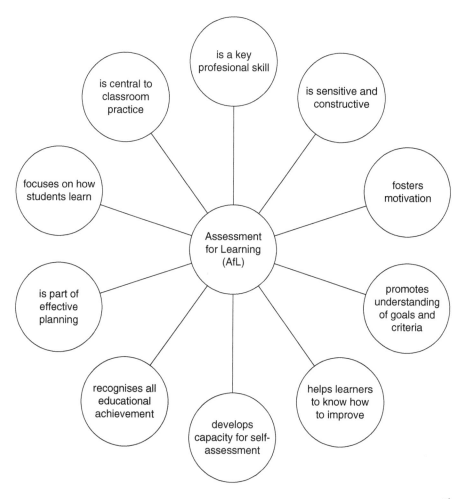

Figure 7.1

WHAT IS ASSESSMENT FOR LEARNING?

Assessment for learning is assessment that promotes learning. It is usually informal and continuous, as well as placing emphasis on advancing learning rather than measuring achievement. It has been argued that:

> *Assessment that is for learning, as opposed to merely of learning, looks forward as well as back. Teachers who assess in this way are concerned not just to confirm and verify what their students have learnt, but also to help their students and themselves understand what the next steps in learning should be and how they might be attempted. This kind of assessment has a 'formative' purpose: it helps to shape what lies ahead rather than simply to gauge and record past achievements.*
>
> (Flórez and Sammons, 2013, p2)

A MODEL OF ASSESSMENT FOR LEARNING

The Assessment Reform Group identified ten principles of assessment for learning (ARG, 2002), which are presented in the following diagram (Figure 7.1).

A CYCLE OF ASSESSMENT

Assessment, planning, teaching and learning are all related in a cycle. This is represented as follows (Figure 7.2).

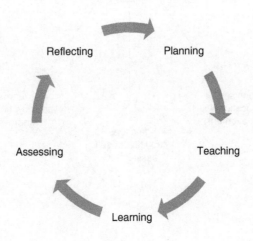

Figure 7.2

ASSESSMENT FOR LEARNING DURING LESSONS

Assessment for learning needs to be integrated into lessons to promote learning. It enables teachers to check understanding, identify and address misconceptions, and modify teaching so that children can make progress. It takes a variety of forms, including questioning, feedback, and self and peer assessment.

BUILDING ASSESSMENT TASKS INTO LESSONS

One assessment for learning strategy is to integrate mini assessment tasks into lessons. These tasks enable teachers to check understanding at specific stages during a lesson. They provide information to the teacher about pupils' understanding so that lessons can be adjusted if pupils have not understood what they have just been taught. If pupils' responses to a task indicate that they have developed misconceptions, the teacher can address these through providing additional support to specific pupils or by reteaching the content in a different way. In this way, the teacher uses the outcomes of the assessment to inform their teaching during the lesson.

Assessment for learning tasks can include quizzes or questions that pupils complete individually, in pairs or in groups. They are usually short tasks that are specifically planned to enable the teacher to check pupils' understanding before moving on to a different stage in the lesson. They can be planned:

- at the start of a lesson to check pupils' understanding of subject content that was taught in a previous lesson;

- after new learning has been modelled and explained;

- throughout the lesson;

- at the end of a lesson.

If the feedback from these tasks indicates that many children have not understood the subject content, the content may need to be retaught to everyone. However, if specific children demonstrate that they have not understood the subject content, these pupils can be targeted individually or in a small group during the lesson so that their misconceptions can be addressed.

QUESTIONING

Research has found that the questions used by teachers are often insufficiently challenging for students (Flórez and Sammons, 2013). In addition, studies have found that the time given to elaborate on an answer is often too short (Condie et al., 2005; Gipps et al., 2005; Kellard et al., 2008; Kirton et al., 2007; Webb and Jones, 2009). Research has recommended increasing the time given for students to think of an answer (Webb and Jones, 2009) and making greater use of open questions rather than closed questions (MacPhail and Halbert, 2010) to promote higher-order thinking. Creating a positive classroom climate in which misconceptions are addressed enables students to learn from mistakes (Torrance and Pryor, 2001) and promotes learning.

Specific questions should be planned to check pupils' understanding or to promote thinking. Questions that require pupils to give more detailed or multiple responses than a single correct answer are more effective at promoting thinking (MacPhail and Halbert, 2010).

Bloom's (1956) taxonomy of thinking skills is a useful framework to support teachers in planning questions. The framework moves from lower-level thinking to higher-level thinking. The lowest level of thinking, according to the framework, is knowledge. Questions to assess knowledge might include:

- What happened after ...?

- How many ...?

- Who was it that ...?

- Can you name the ...?

- Describe what happened at ...

- Who spoke to ...?

- What is the meaning of ...?

- What is ...?

- Which is true or false ...?

The next level of thinking is understanding. Questions to assess understanding might include:

- Can you explain ...?

- What are the differences between ...?

- Who was the key character in this story and why?

The next level of thinking is application. This relates to the ability to apply knowledge to different contexts. Questions to assess application might include:

- Why do you think wet clothes dry on a washing line?

- Why do the light bulbs on one floor in a house go out but they stay lit on a different floor?

- Can you solve this word problem using your knowledge of division?

The next level of thinking is analysis. Questions to assess analysis might include:

- How is … similar to …?

- Can you distinguish between … and …?

- How has the author used description to show how the character is feeling?

- Why do you think the author used this word?

- What effect might the author's choice of words have on the reader?

The next level of thinking is evaluating. Questions to develop the skill of evaluation might include:

- Having considered the arguments for and against … what do you think about this?

- What sort of character is X and how do you know?

The highest level of thinking is creating. This is where pupils use their knowledge and understanding to create something. Questions might include:

- Can you design …?

- Can you build …?

- Can you construct …?

ADDRESSING MISCONCEPTIONS

There are various ways to address misconceptions during lessons. One strategy that some teachers use is to research common misconceptions relating to subject content and then highlight these explicitly to pupils during the teaching of subject content. Questioning is a very effective strategy for identifying and unpicking misconceptions in knowledge or understanding. Teachers can also observe pupils as they are working to identify misconceptions. Misconceptions can be addressed in a range of ways. These include:

- reteaching subject content;

- rephrasing or re-explaining something;

- providing individual support to pupils during lessons;

- highlighting misconceptions to the whole class;

- providing support to small groups of pupils who develop common misconceptions.

SELF-ASSESSMENT

Research has demonstrated how self-assessment can promote metacognitive skills (Brookhart, 2001; Gipps et al., 2005; Stiggins and Arter, 2002). During the process of self-assessment, pupils learn to evaluate their work in relation to the expected outcomes. They identify what they have achieved in relation to the original goals and aspects that strengthen the work. This process of evaluating learning is critical to becoming a good learner.

The process of self-assessment should be ongoing. It should take place during the process of completing a task in addition to taking place when the task is finished. This helps pupils to evaluate their work as they go along and adjust it to make improvements. Self-evaluation is generally more effective if pupils are clear from the outset about the criteria for assessment. One way of addressing this is to provide pupils with a checklist so that they know what aspects to include in their work. This works particularly well in writing tasks.

PEER ASSESSMENT

Research demonstrates that pupils generally are more accepting of feedback from their peers rather than feedback from their teachers (Flórez and Sammons, 2013). Teachers need to carefully consider the pairings that are used during the process of peer assessment. One strategy that might be adopted is to pair children together who are working at different stages of development. A decision will also need to be made about whether the pairings will be consistent across the academic year or whether different pairings will be used so that children gain feedback from other peers across the year. Children will also need to be trained in the process of peer assessment. They need to understand the purposes of peer assessment and how to give feedback. Teachers need to establish a supportive classroom climate so that all pupils view peer feedback as a supportive and developmental process.

MARKING

Marking pupils' work enables you to check their understanding of the subject content. It also informs what you do subsequently in the next lesson. If pupils have not understood an aspect of subject content, you will need to revisit this in the next lesson, particularly if many pupils have developed misconceptions. You will need to adopt the marking policy of the school. Essentially, written feedback should be brief and specific. It should communicate to pupils what they have done well and what they need to improve. It should be aligned with the intended learning outcomes rather than focusing on everything.

Many schools are now taking steps to reduce teacher workload in relation to marking. It is not necessary to mark every single piece of work in detail and it is not always necessary to mark every child's exercise book. It is possible to mark a selection of books to identify misconceptions, which can then be addressed with the whole class in the next lesson. Sometimes it will be necessary to conduct detailed marking of specific pieces of work, but it is unmanageable to do this for every piece of work. One way of reducing workload is to mark work with the children during the lesson. This provides them with immediate feedback in relation to how well they are doing.

FEEDBACK

Feedback should provide the following information (Figure 7.3).

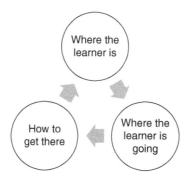

Figure 7.3

Research from Hattie and Timperley (2007) suggests that models of feedback should address three questions:

- Where am I going?

- How am I doing?

- Where to next?

According to Hattie and Timperley (2007), the answers to these questions enhance learning when there is a discrepancy between what is understood and what is aimed at being understood. It can increase effort, motivation or engagement to reduce this discrepancy, and/or it can increase cue searching and task processes that lead to understanding (thus reducing this discrepancy). Feedback is among the most critical influences on student learning. A major aim of the educative process is to assist in identifying these gaps ('How am I doing?' relative to 'Where am I going?') and to provide remediation in the form of alternative or other steps ('Where to next?').

Feedback comments should be specific rather than general. Comments such as 'good work' are unhelpful because they do not communicate to pupils why the work is good. More specific praise is beneficial (e.g. 'You have used some good imperative verbs in these written instructions').

Good-quality feedback is an essential aspect of assessment for learning (MacPhail and Halbert, 2010). Seminal research found that when students were given comment-only feedback rather than assigning marks or grades, they subsequently did better in achievement tests (Butler, 1987). Informative and descriptive feedback is more effective than simply marking students' work as correct or incorrect (Flórez and Sammons, 2013). This is because marking students' work as right or wrong can promote competition between students, which can damage the self-esteem of students who get low scores.

Feedback should provide pupils with guidelines not only about what is incorrect in their work, but also on what has been done correctly in relation to the initial learning goals or expectations. Explicit guidance on what they can do to improve and keep on progressing towards expectations is also essential. This feedback practice promotes greater motivation and commitment to enhancing their own learning than feedback where work is marked as either correct or incorrect and where marks are then assigned (Flórez and Sammons, 2013).

USING ASSESSMENT TO INFORM PLANNING

Your assessments will inform you about pupils' knowledge and understanding. If your assessments during lessons indicate that pupils have developed misconceptions, then it will be necessary to adjust the lesson 'on the spot' to address these. If the marking process indicates that pupils have developed misconceptions, you will need to adjust your lesson plan for the subsequent lesson to address these misconceptions. In these ways, assessment for learning informs the teacher about what they need to do next, as well as informing the child.

TAKE 5

- Use live marking to reduce your workload and provide immediate feedback.
- Plan for and deliver mini assessment tasks throughout your lessons.
- Offer informative and descriptive feedback before releasing marks and grades or confirming whether children's work is correct.

- Use pupil checklists so that they know what to include in their work.

- Use open questions and ensure that you offer enough time for children to formulate a response or solution.

CLASSROOM EXAMPLE

Before you begin to mark children's work, it is important that you are clear about what it is you are trying to achieve and the best way of achieving it. You are the most important person in deciding how to give effective feedback to your learners. For example, when you are trying to identify misconceptions, it is appropriate to sample a range of exercise books and identify common themes. You can then address these through whole-class feedback, and in doing so avoid marking the exercise book of every child. Equally, in some cases, you may decide that it is important to mark a piece of written work in depth for every child.

WHAT DOES GOOD PRACTICE IN ASSESSMENT FOR LEARNING LOOK LIKE IN THE CLASSROOM?

The time taken to mark pieces of work does not always correlate with pupil achievement. Avoid providing written dialogue when a conversation can be used instead, and do not provide extensive commentary on children's work when it is not required. Instead, identify meaningful and impactful approaches to the sharing of feedback in a way that reduces your workload while maintaining or improving the quality of feedback offered.

CHAPTER CHECKLIST

	Accessed	Secure	Confident
Know that:			
assessment for learning includes key approaches that I can identify			
Know how to:			
use questioning both to check understanding and promote thinking			

(Continued)

(Continued)

	Accessed	Secure	Confident
use assessment tasks in lessons to check pupils' understanding			
use peer assessment			
use self-assessment			
use effective feedback in lessons			
mark children's work in line with the school policy			
provide written feedback to children			
use formative assessment to inform planning and teaching			
use summative assessment data to inform planning			

8

BEHAVIOUR

┌─ **IN THIS CHAPTER** ──────────────────────────────────

This chapter introduces you to key research on behaviour management. It emphasises the importance of teaching learning behaviours and managing misbehaviours, as well as the value of consistent and clear behaviour policies. Throughout the chapter, practical guidance is offered to support you to teach good learning behaviours and to use rules and routines, as well as praise, rewards and sanctions, effectively. The chapter argues that children's behaviour is influenced by multiple and interrelated factors, and that knowing your pupils well can support you to have a positive impact on classroom behaviour. Effective practice is illustrated through case studies.

KEY RESEARCH

The outcomes of several research studies into behaviour suggest that the following strategies are important in supporting pupils' behaviour:

- knowing and understanding your pupils and their influences;

- teaching learning behaviours alongside managing misbehaviour;

- using classroom management strategies to support good classroom behaviour;

- being consistent;

- having a clear behaviour policy;

- using targeted approaches to meet the needs of individuals.

(EEF, 2019)

KEY POLICY

The teachers' standards state that teachers must:

- have clear rules and routines for behaviour in classrooms, as well as taking responsibility for promoting good and courteous behaviour both in classrooms and around the school, in accordance with the school behaviour policy;

- have high expectations of behaviour, as well as establishing a framework for discipline with a range of strategies, using praise, sanctions and rewards consistently and fairly;

- manage classes effectively, using approaches that are appropriate to pupils' needs in order to involve and motivate them;

- maintain good relationships with pupils, exercise appropriate authority, and act decisively when necessary.

(DfE, 2011)

The Department for Education states that:

- Teachers have statutory authority to discipline pupils whose behaviour is unacceptable, who break the school rules or who fail to follow a reasonable instruction (Education and Inspections Act 2006, sections 90 and 91) (HM Government, 2006).

- The power also applies to all paid staff (unless the head teacher says otherwise) with responsibility for pupils, such as teaching assistants.

- Teachers can discipline pupils at any time the pupil is in school or elsewhere under the charge of a teacher, including on school visits.

- Teachers can also discipline pupils in certain circumstances when a pupil's misbehaviour occurs outside of school.

- Teachers have the power to impose detention outside school hours. This would not typically be used in primary schools.

- Teachers can confiscate pupils' property.

(DfE, 2016)

WHAT IS BEHAVIOUR?

Children's behaviour is influenced by a variety of biological and environmental factors. We view behaviours as an attempt to communicate an unmet need and as a form of communication. Through their behaviours, children are often trying to communicate something to others. It is important to recognise that some children may need to learn the boundaries of acceptable and unacceptable behaviours, particularly if they have been exposed to inappropriate behaviours and inconsistent expectations in their families and communities.

KNOWING YOUR PUPILS AND BUILDING RELATIONSHIPS

Supportive relationships are a key motivation for teachers joining the profession (Day et al., 2006). Research suggests that teachers knowing their pupils well can have a positive impact on classroom behaviour (Sammons et al., 2016). Children's behaviour is influenced by multiple factors, including influences from family, school and community contexts, as well as biological factors. Research suggests that multiple and interrelated factors influence each child's developmental course and academic growth (Chodkiewicz and Boyle, 2017).

Challenging experiences for pupils at home or in the community can negatively affect their ability to learn or cope with the school environment, which could lead to disengagement from learning (Chodkiewicz and Boyle, 2016). For example, there is a growing body of research that identifies the harmful effects of adverse childhood experiences (ACEs) on long-term life outcomes. ACEs are significant stressful events occurring during childhood or adolescence. They can include but are not limited to child abuse, parental conflict, parental substance abuse, and poor parental mental health (EEF, 2019). These factors can influence the child's behaviour. In addition, a key influence on a child's behaviour in school is being the victim of bullying (Brown, 2018). It is therefore critical that schools have robust policies to address bullying so that children can learn in a safe environment.

When teachers understand the influences on children's behaviour, they can support them more effectively. Some children are not exposed to models of good behaviour in their homes and communities. They may need a social and emotional curriculum (Roffey, 2017) through which they can learn to adapt their social behaviours according to the contexts they are in. Through the explicit teaching of social and emotional skills, they can also learn to name, recognise and regulate their emotions.

It is critical that children know that you like them, and crucially that you are on their side. They need to know that you believe in them and that you will forgive them for the times that they demonstrate inappropriate behaviour. They need you to respond with empathy and kindness even when they do not demonstrate this to you. You need to remember that you are the adult in this relationship and that they are still learning. Strategies for establishing effective relationships include:

- knowing their names;

- smiling at them;

- communicating their strengths to them;

- giving them responsibilities in the classroom;

- being prepared to forgive them;

- using praise;

- demonstrating that you believe in them.

TEACH LEARNING BEHAVIOURS

Research suggests that when children improve their learning behaviours, this skill set can improve both academic achievement and cognitive ability.

A learning behaviour is a behaviour that is necessary for a child to learn effectively in the classroom (Ellis and Tod, 2018). Research suggests that teaching learning behaviours explicitly reduces the need for teachers to constantly 'manage' misbehaviour (Bitsika, 2003). Research suggests that when children improve their learning behaviours, this skill set can improve both academic achievement and cognitive ability (McDermott et al., 2001). Some children come to school with limited understanding of what constitutes appropriate behaviour. They may have been raised in families and communities where inappropriate behaviour is the norm and they may not have been provided with clear behaviour boundaries.

As a teacher, it is important not to assume that children will automatically understand what is meant by good behaviour in general, and they may need to be taught about what constitutes good learning behaviours. Good learning behaviours include:

- listening;
- concentrating;
- persevering;
- asking questions;
- collaborating;
- managing distractions;
- being independent.

This is not an exhaustive list, and you will be able to add to it. You may need to explicitly teach your pupils about the characteristics of a good learner. These behaviours can be reinforced by providing children with specific descriptive praise when they demonstrate them (e.g. 'Well done, Mohammed, you are persevering with that problem').

RULES AND ROUTINES

Good behaviour in classrooms is promoted through rules and routines. It is better to phrase rules in positive language (e.g. using the phrase 'We listen when others are talking' rather than 'Do not interrupt'). It is good practice to involve the class in generating the classroom rules. This provides them with ownership by allowing children to shape the 'behaviour contact'.

Clear routines provide children with security. These might include:

- agreed ways of entering and leaving the classroom;
- consistent tasks that children complete at specific times of the day;
- a consistent timetable;
- consistent signals for gaining attention;
- consistency in lesson structure.

USING PRAISE

Everyone enjoys receiving praise and there is a general assumption that praise serves a motivating function. However, Coe et al. (2014) cite studies which demonstrate that the wrong kinds of praise can be detrimental, particularly if praise is not genuinely deserved and actually communicates low teacher expectations. It is also important to make sure that all children receive praise. It is too easy to praise children who typically demonstrate inappropriate behaviour when we suddenly see them behaving well. There is a risk that children who always behave appropriately miss out on praise because teachers just expect them to behave well.

REWARDS

Through operant conditioning, a child makes an association between a behaviour and a consequence (Skinner, 1938). The underlying principle is that positive reinforcement of good behaviour strengthens that behaviour. We have represented operant conditioning in the model below (Figure 8.1).

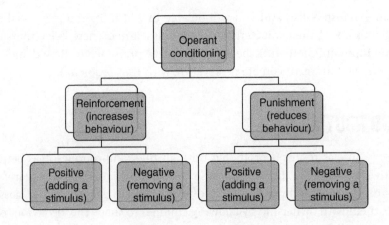

Figure 8.1

Reinforcements seek to increase desired behaviour. Examples include:

- *Positive reinforcement.* Issuing praise or a tangible reward so that the behaviour is repeated.

- *Negative reinforcement.* Taking something away that is undesirable to increase positive behaviour (e.g. removing an autistic child from a noisy environment that is causing distress).

Negative reinforcement is often confused with punishment (see below), which is incorrect.

In contrast, punishment seeks to reduce undesirable behaviour. Examples include:

- *Positive punishment.* Introducing a sanction to reduce poor behaviour.

- *Negative punishment.* Removing a potentially rewarding stimulus (e.g. loss of privileges or loss of break time).

Rewarding good behaviour can motivate children to repeat that behaviour but rewards can promote extrinsic motivation. Although rewards can be useful to address some minor misbehaviours or encourage positive behaviour, research suggests that children who are intrinsically motivated achieve better and are less likely to misbehave (EEF, 2019).

GROWTH MINDSET

Carol Dweck's research on 'growth mindset' suggests that intelligence is not a fixed characteristic, but can instead be increased through effort. Dweck (2008) suggests that teaching children to have this mindset can motivate them not only to improve academically, but also to behave better.

SANCTIONS

Most school behaviour policies include consequences or sanctions that are issued when the classroom or school rules are broken. The Department for Education guidelines state that:

> A punishment must be proportionate. In determining whether a punishment is reasonable, section 91 of the Education and Inspections Act 2006 says the penalty must be reasonable in all the circumstances and that account must be taken of the pupil's age, any special educational needs or disability they may have, and any religious requirements affecting them.

> (DfE, 2016, p7)

In primary schools, sanctions might include the following:

- a verbal reprimand;

- loss of privileges;

- missing break time or staying in at lunchtime;

- in more extreme cases, schools may use temporary or permanent exclusion.

REASONABLE FORCE

Teachers are allowed to use reasonable force to respond to incidents of behaviour. The Department for Education guidelines state that:

> Members of staff have the power to use reasonable force to prevent pupils committing an offence, injuring themselves or others, or damaging property, and to maintain good order and discipline in the classroom.

> (DfE, 2016, p12)

However, the problem with this guidance is that the term 'reasonable' is not adequately defined; it can mean different things to different people, and consequently the lack of definition can leave teachers vulnerable, especially if a parent or a child perceives that the force used was not reasonable. Staff who are employed within schools undertake training in handling techniques. These techniques enable staff to move children safely in situations where children become a danger to themselves and others.

DIFFUSING SITUATIONS

As a teacher, it is almost inevitable that you will experience some difficult behaviours during your time in the classroom. These can sometimes develop and escalate quickly, and it is important that you are able to act quickly and decisively in order to attempt to restore calm and order. There are a range of strategies and approaches that you may find useful to diffuse these situations. These include:

- adopting a confident body posture;

- tactically ignoring secondary behaviours and remaining focused on the issue that you are already dealing with;

- using children's names to maintain attention and reiterate the existing relationship you may already have with them;

- reinforcing school policies to make it clear that your approach is not a personal attack;

- circulating the room;

- addressing inappropriate behaviour as soon as you see it so that it does not escalate;

- distracting the child;

- removing the child from an area where potential conflict may arise and taking them to another area to complete a task for you;

- staying calm;

- dealing with behaviour quietly in order to reduce the involvement of additional children;

- coming down to talk to children at their level to provide a sense of safety.

It is also important to acknowledge that there may be some situations which you cannot deal with on your own, and you should not attempt to do so. Equally, you cannot control children's behaviour, and in some cases attempts to diffuse a situation may not be successful. If a child refuses to follow your instruction and leave the classroom, you may find it helpful to calmly ask the rest of the children to leave and line up outside so that they are removed from the environment.

DEALING WITH CHALLENGING BEHAVIOUR

It is the responsibility of school leaders to develop a whole-school approach to promoting positive behaviour. However, despite being proactive and adopting these preventative measures, occasions will still arise when it is necessary for you to respond to and address challenging behaviour within the classroom.

It is essential that school policy is adhered to when dealing with challenging behaviour. In addition to following your school policy, there are a range of strategies and approaches you can use to support you. These include:

- phrasing instructions and commands positively (e.g. 'Thank you for stopping talking, Jonathan' rather than 'Stop talking, Jonathan');

- addressing misbehaviour respectfully in a way that minimises class disruption and encourages discussion;

- enforcing consequences at a later stage to prevent escalation in the short term;

- remaining calm and controlling your emotions and aggression;

- maintaining a safe distance between yourself and the child at all times to ensure that your actions are not perceived as a physical threat;

- providing opportunities for children to calm down before attempting to discuss behaviour incidents.

You may find it helpful to discuss these with colleagues. It is important to remember that seeking advice and support from colleagues is never a sign of weakness.

When dealing with a situation, it is important to wait for the child to calm down before you try to discuss the incident with them. Throughout the discussion, you must remain calm and composed in order to effectively convey the points you need to discuss.

TAKE 5

- Learn children's names and use these regularly to support you to establish relationships.

- Plan and teach learning behaviours explicitly.

- Use rules and routines regularly and consistently to promote good behaviour.

- Phrase your instructions positively to assume, rather than request, compliance.

- Deal with all behaviour incidents calmly and consistently.

CLASSROOM EXAMPLE

If you ask a child to move from one seat to another and they refuse, you must stay calm. Repeat your instruction quietly and provide the child with take-up time to comply with your request. Try to maintain your immediate focus on encouraging the child to comply with your original instruction rather than any secondary behaviours they may be displaying. Try to maintain ownership of the situation, although you must involve a colleague when it is necessary to do so. At this stage, it may be appropriate to move the class to another location. At all times apply your school behaviour policy and document the child's responses. This will allow you to enforce consequences when it is appropriate to do so, as it is essential that children are held accountable for their behaviour. It will also support you to hold a meaningful conversation with parents and discuss the behaviours that you witnessed.

WHAT DOES GOOD PRACTICE IN SUPPORTING BEHAVIOUR LOOK LIKE IN THE CLASSROOM?

Set clear and consistent expectations in order to support children to understand how they are expected to behave. These may be communicated verbally and supported through a display within your classroom that you can refer to at a later stage. This will help children to remember what is expected of them. Try to use words such as 'we' rather than 'you' in order to create a sense of belonging and community within the learning space.

CHAPTER CHECKLIST

	Accessed	Secure	Confident
Know that:			
a variety of factors influence children's behaviour			
there are a variety of strategies to support children's behaviour, but children will respond differently to them			
Know how to:			
establish effective relationships with children			
use praise effectively			

	Accessed	Secure	Confident
use sanctions appropriately			
use diffusion strategies			
establish rules and routines to create a sense of security			

9
METACOGNITION

┌─ IN THIS CHAPTER ───┐

This chapter introduces you to key research on metacognition. It emphasises the impact
of metacognitive and self-regulation approaches in relation to pupil achievement and outcomes, and the key features of each approach are highlighted. Throughout the chapter,
practical guidance is offered to enable you to embed metacognitive approaches within
your classroom by supporting children to plan, monitor and evaluate their own learning.
The chapter argues that self-reflection is a critical aspect of metacognition, and the role
of challenge and scaffolding is also outlined in relation to metacognition. Effective practice is illustrated through case studies.

└───┘

KEY RESEARCH

Research findings suggest that:

- Metacognition and self-regulation approaches have consistently high levels of impact,
  with pupils making an average of seven months' additional progress.

- These strategies are usually more effective when taught in collaborative groups so that
  learners can support each other and make their thinking explicit through discussion.

- The potential impact of these approaches is high but can be difficult to achieve in practice, as they require pupils to take greater responsibility for their learning and develop
  their understanding of what is required to succeed.

- The evidence indicates that teaching these strategies can be particularly effective for
  low-achieving and older pupils.

(EEF, 2018)

Metacognition and self-regulation approaches have consistently high levels of impact,
with pupils making an average of seven months' additional progress (Higgins et al., 2014).
Metacognitive strategies help students think about their own learning more explicitly by
teaching them specific strategies for planning, monitoring and evaluating their learning.

KEY POLICY

The Initial Teacher Training (ITT) core content framework states that trainee teachers must learn that:

> *Explicitly teaching pupils metacognitive strategies linked to subject knowledge, including how to plan, monitor and evaluate, supports independence and academic success.*

(DfE, 2019b, p17)

WHAT IS METACOGNITION?

In brief, metacognition involves the skills of setting goals, planning, organising and evaluating performance, monitoring progress, and reflecting on your own learning.

A MODEL OF METACOGNITION

The metacognitive learner broadly adopts the following cycle (Figure 9.1).

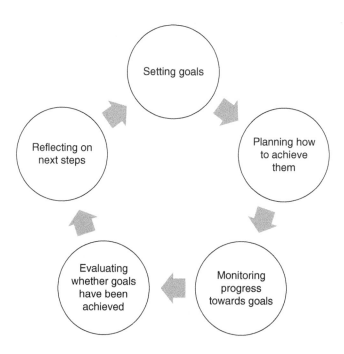

Figure 9.1

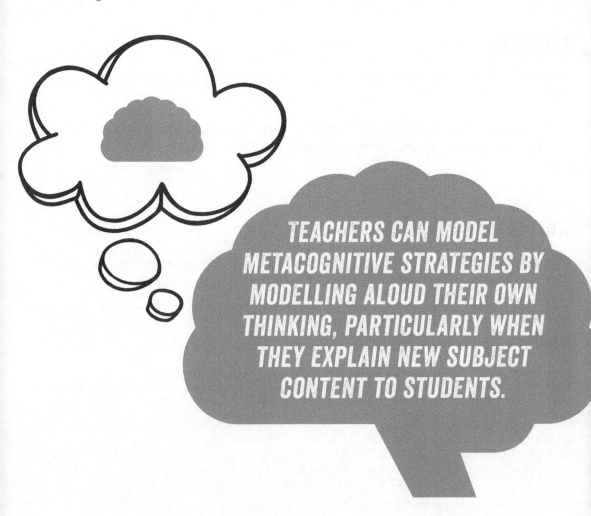

TEACHERS CAN MODEL METACOGNITIVE STRATEGIES BY MODELLING ALOUD THEIR OWN THINKING, PARTICULARLY WHEN THEY EXPLAIN NEW SUBJECT CONTENT TO STUDENTS.

WHAT DO WE MEAN BY METACOGNITION AND SELF-REGULATION?

Metacognition is the process of 'thinking about one's own thinking' (Georghiades, 2004, p365). It facilitates a deeper conceptual understanding of content and more strategic learning. Students who have good metacognitive skills can effectively monitor their own learning, regulate their own behaviour, set themselves goals, monitor their own achievement towards these, and evaluate their own progress.

Research has found that students who employ metacognitive strategies, including self-regulated learning and goal setting, are more able to engage in cognitive processes and remember information, as well as having greater capacity for learning (Farrington et al., 2012).

Teachers can model metacognitive strategies by modelling aloud their own thinking, particularly when they explain new subject content to students. Metacognitive abilities can also enhance motivation (Cantor et al., 2019) because students are aware of their own goals, strengths and weaknesses, and can evaluate their own learning in relation to their goals.

According to the Education Endowment Foundation:

> *Metacognition and self-regulation approaches aim to help pupils think about their own learning more explicitly, often by teaching them specific strategies for planning, monitoring and evaluating their learning. Interventions are usually designed to give pupils a repertoire of strategies to choose from and the skills to select the most suitable strategy for a given learning task.*
>
> (EEF, 2018)

Essentially, self-regulation is about the extent to which pupils are aware of their strengths and weaknesses, as well as the strategies they use to learn. Self-regulated learners can motivate themselves to engage in learning and develop strategies to improve their learning. Self-regulated learners are:

- proactive in their efforts to learn;

- aware of their own strengths and weaknesses;

- good at setting their own goals to enhance their learning;

- able to check the accuracy of their work;

- able to monitor their progress towards their goals;

- able to self-reflect on their learning;

- motivated to continue to improve.

(Zimmerman, 2010)

Self-regulation in learning involves cognition, metacognition and motivation:

- *Cognition* refers to the mental process involved in knowing and understanding a subject, as well as the ability to grasp subject-specific skills. Cognitive strategies include skills such as memorisation techniques or subject-specific strategies.

- *Metacognition* is about the ways that pupils monitor and purposefully direct their learning (e.g. the skills of planning, monitoring and evaluating their learning, as well as making adaptations to improve their performance). Metacognitive strategies enable pupils to monitor or control their cognition.

- *Motivation* relates to pupils' willingness to engage their metacognitive and cognitive skills. Motivational strategies include investing effort and perseverance into a task, as well as convincing oneself that a task needs to be completed.

PLANNING LEARNING

Effective learners can plan their learning by breaking down tasks into smaller parts. They can order these parts into a logical sequence so that they know what steps to complete first, second, third, and so on. They can set themselves goals so that they know what they want to achieve within a specific timescale. Providing children with writing frames is a useful strategy to support them to plan their writing. Writing frames (or graphic organisers) can support pupils to think carefully about the different structural and language features of specific text types. They can then use the plan that they have produced on the writing frame to structure their writing. Writing frames can also be used to support pupils to plan their writing in other subjects (e.g. pupils can use graphic organisers in science to support them in writing scientific explanations and reports of scientific investigations). Pupils can plan the vocabulary they intend to use in their creative writing before they start the process of writing. They can plan the steps that they need to follow to produce a product in design and technology before they start writing. These are all different examples of how teachers can support pupils to plan their learning.

MONITORING LEARNING

Effective learners can monitor their own learning. The process of monitoring learning is ongoing and takes place during a task. Children with good metacognitive skills can identify whether they are achieving their intended goals, whether their work is good enough, or whether they need to adapt it during the process of completing a task. This process of monitoring helps children to improve the quality of their work so that they achieve their goals.

One strategy for supporting learners to monitor their learning is to teach them to check their work during a task. This works particularly well in mathematics (e.g. children can be taught strategies to check the accuracy of a mathematical calculation by using an inverse calculation). In this way, pupils can use different calculation strategies to check their answers to mathematical problems. Another strategy is to provide children with 'steps to success' through a mathematical problem. Children follow the steps sequentially to complete the problem and then work through them again to check the accuracy of their answers. In English, teachers can provide children with checklists that identify the aspects of grammar, sentence structure, vocabulary and punctuation which must be present in a piece of writing. Children can then use the checklist during the writing task to check that they are including all of the required features. If children start to monitor their learning during a task, this will help them to identify how to improve their work before the work is completed.

EVALUATING LEARNING

Children with good metacognitive skills can evaluate their work. Teachers can support this process of evaluation using a range of pedagogical approaches. These might include:

- providing children with clear success criteria to support evaluation;

- asking children to self-assess their work against the success criteria;

- sharing models of good work with the class and asking them to evaluate their work against this;

- introducing peer assessment;

- asking children to identify what aspects of their work are good and to identify one aspect for improvement;

- modelling correct or good responses on the screen/whiteboard and asking pupils to evaluate their work in relation to the model;

- asking pupils to reflect on the learning process (e.g. how well they worked as part of a team);

- meeting children once every half-term to engage them in reflecting on their strengths and weaknesses.

STRUCTURED REFLECTION

Providing opportunities for pupils to reflect on their work and themselves as learners is a critical aspect of metacognition. Children can be supported in this process by providing them with a set of questions or prompts that help to structure their reflections. Children need to understand that reflection is a key component of effective learning and that good learners are always seeking ways to improve. Other strategies for facilitating reflection include:

- pupils writing a reflective comment at the end of a piece of work;

- asking pupils to reflect on three things that they have achieved in their learning each week and one thing that they want to improve on the following week;

- pupils keeping a reflective diary over the duration of a year that includes evidence of their achievements (e.g. photographs of their learning and written reflections).

MODELLING THINKING ALOUD

If we want children to be authors, historians or mathematicians, for example, they need to understand how these people think. One way of helping children to start thinking as authors, historians or mathematicians is to model the process of thinking aloud. Teachers can do this during the process of modelling subject-specific content. If a teacher is modelling composition in writing, for example, it is important to support children to consider audience. In other words, children need to understand how writers use specific features in their writing to have an impact on the reader. This process is known as 'writing as a reader'. So, let's imagine you are modelling writing a story. You might start writing the first few lines of the story, but as you do this you also verbalise your thinking. For example, you might say the following as you are writing:

- 'I need an adjective to go in front of this noun to give the reader some detail.'

- 'I am going to change this word for a better word because it gives the reader more information.'

- 'I want to include some dialogue to keep the reader engaged.'

- 'I am going to go back through this writing and change some words to make it more powerful.'

- 'I've used this word, but it's boring. Can we think of a better word?'

This strategy of thinking aloud makes explicit to children the type of thinking that you want them to demonstrate in their own work. Consider now how this approach might be used in other subjects.

ADDING IN DELIBERATE DIFFICULTY

The tasks that you set the pupils should neither be too easy nor too hard. If they are too easy, there is no cognitive demand. If they are too difficult, the cognitive load might be too great. Aim to pitch the learning at a level above the level that the child is operating at. The level should be appropriate and achievable for the child with the support of the teacher. The following process is a useful way of thinking about lesson structure:

- Activate prior learning.

- Model the new learning.

- Introduce guided learning. This is where you support the pupils to complete the task or they support each other to complete it.

- Implement independent learning.

- Check throughout the lesson and at the end of the lesson that the pupils have understood.

REMOVING THE SCAFFOLDING

Providing children with scaffolding can support them to reach a higher level of development. Scaffolds can take many forms, including adult support, resources and writing frames. If pupils rely on these scaffolds for too long, there is a danger that they become dependent on them and they can restrict their independence. It is therefore important to gradually remove the scaffolds so that pupils can achieve independence in learning.

METACOGNITIVE TALK IN THE CLASSROOM

Metacognitive classroom talk is talk that promotes learning. Alexander (2017) emphasises the importance of dialogic teaching. This strategy emphasises classroom dialogue through which pupils learn to reason, discuss, argue and explain. According to Alexander (2017), the most effective classroom talk strategies for developing metacognitive skills are:

- *Learning talk.* This includes narrating, questioning and discussing.

- *Teaching talk.* This includes instruction, exposition and dialogue.

Alexander (2017) argues that both discussion and dialogue are powerful, but not common in classrooms, and therefore need to be given much greater prominence.

TAKE 5

- Ask children to set themselves goals so that they know what they want to achieve within a specific timescale.

- Encourage children to check the accuracy of their work (e.g. through the use of inverse calculations in mathematics).

- Provide children with clear success criteria to support self-reflection and self-evaluation.

- Model the process of thinking to help children to start thinking as authors, historians or mathematicians, for example.

- Gradually remove scaffolds to promote children's independence in learning.

CLASSROOM EXAMPLE

Teach children basic skills and then set them a task or activity that requires the application of these skills to an unknown or unfamiliar problem or scenario. For example, teach children a specific mathematical skill and then present a problem-based scenario that draws on this specific skill. This will require children to think about what they already know and how this can be applied to the problem. This is the planning stage. While working through the problem, they will then monitor their progress by asking themselves whether they have correctly applied the skill to the problem or scenario. Once a solution has been found, children can evaluate their work using an inverse calculation or worked answer.

WHAT DOES GOOD PRACTICE IN METACOGNITION LOOK LIKE IN THE CLASSROOM?

Metacognitive practices have been shown to improve academic achievement across a range of ages, cognitive abilities and learning domains. It is therefore important that the following aspects of metacognition are used to inform and support planning and delivery:

- *Metacognitive knowledge.* The learner's knowledge of their own cognitive abilities.

- *Metacognitive regulation.* How learners monitor and control their cognitive processes (e.g. realising that the strategy they are using to solve a mathematical problem is not working and then using an alternative approach).

- *Metacognitive practices.* Helping learners to plan, monitor and evaluate their own progress and take control of their learning as they read, write and solve problems in the classroom.

(Cambridge Assessment, 2019)

CHAPTER CHECKLIST

	Accessed	Secure	Confident
Know that:			
metacognition involves a variety of pedagogical approaches that I can identify			
Know how to:			
support pupils to plan their learning			
support pupils to monitor their learning			
model metacognitive strategies in my own teaching			

CONCLUSION

This book has addressed key aspects of effective primary teaching. It has presented key research findings, and some chapters include links to theories where these are relevant.

The need for evidence-informed approaches to teaching is clear. Evidence provides an underpinning rationale for practice and helps teachers to defend the approaches that they choose to use. More importantly, evidence-informed teaching supports children's learning. It is, however, important to recognise that 'what works' in one context may not work in another. Schools are vastly different and so are children. What works in one school or with one child may not work in or with another. That said, we can learn lessons from research that might usefully inform our practice in the classroom.

We end this book by returning to a concept that we stated in the introduction: the teacher as a 'consumer' of research (Carter, 2015). Instead, we wish to reposition the teacher to one of 'producer' of research. We believe that the work teachers are undertaking in the classroom is valuable research, and as such in this conclusion we wish to leave the reader to consider the concept of practice-informed research rather than research-informed practice, even though this is not something we have addressed throughout the book.

Philpott and Poultney's (2018) book *Evidence-Based Teaching* makes several critical arguments. They argue that there is a need to develop a deeper understanding of the value of practitioner investigation as an integral part of academic research. This move towards practice-informed research rather than research-informed practice requires teachers to critically engage with evidence from their own practice to determine 'what works' in specific school contexts. They argue that practitioner research has a central role to play in the health of a school, and that career structures should be developed that value higher-level study and reward teachers accordingly so that teachers can become 'scholars of educational research' (Winch et al., 2015, p213). They highlight the importance of university–school partnerships in developing teachers as researchers, and they argue that a single research method is unlikely to be the best way of investigating practice-based issues.

Philpott and Poultney's book makes an important contribution to the teaching profession through making the case for practice-informed research. Teachers can be empowered to be researchers of their own practice once they recognise that the evidence which naturally emerges from their professional practice are forms of data that can be used to support deep reflection.

We would like to see the teaching profession moving in this direction because not only does this shift in approach provide teachers with agency, but it ensures that research is contextually sensitive and fine-tuned to meet the needs of schools and children. We want to empower teachers to be researchers rather than adopting a model in which professional researchers determine the practices of teachers. Instead, we believe that the practices of teachers should inform the body of research, rather than the other way around.

REFERENCES

Abiola, O.O. and Dhindsa, H.S. (2012) 'Improving classroom practices using our knowledge of how the brain works', *International Journal of Environmental and Science Education*, 7(1): 71–81.

Ainscow, M. (2000) 'Profile', in P. Clough and J. Corbett (eds), *Theories of Inclusive Education: A Students' Guide*, London: Paul Chapman.

Alexander, R.J. (2017) *Towards Dialogic Teaching: Rethinking Classroom Talk* (5th edn), Thirsk: Dialogos.

Allan, J. (1996) 'Foucault and special educational needs: a "box of tools" for analysing children's experiences of mainstreaming', *Disability and Society*, 11(2): 219–33.

Allan, J. (2000) 'Reflection: inconclusive education? Towards settled uncertainty', in P. Clough and J. Corbett (eds), *Theories of Inclusive Education: A Students' Guide*, London: Paul Chapman.

Allan, J. (2006) 'The repetition of exclusion', *International Journal of Inclusive Education*, 10(2/3): 121–33.

Armstrong, D. (2005) 'Reinventing "inclusion": New Labour and the cultural politics of special education', *Oxford Review of Education*, 31(1): 135–51.

Assessment Reform Group (ARG) (2002) *Research-Based Principles of Assessment for Learning to Guide Classroom Practice*, London: ARG.

Avramidis, E., Bayliss, P. and Burden, R. (2002) 'Inclusion in action: an in-depth case study of an effective inclusive secondary school in the south-west of England', *International Journal of Inclusive Education*, 6(2): 143–63.

Azzopardi, A. (2009) *Reading Stories of Inclusion: Engaging with Different Perspectives Towards an Agenda for Inclusion*, Saarbrücken: VDM Verlag Dr. Müller.

Azzopardi, A. (ed.) (2010) *Making Sense of Inclusive Education: Where Everyone Belongs*, Saarbrücken: VDM Verlag Dr. Müller.

Baddeley, A.D. (2000) 'The episodic buffer: a new component of working memory?', *Trends in Cognitive Sciences*, 4(11): 417–23.

Baddeley, A.D. and Hitch, G.J. (1974) 'Working memory', in G.A. Bower (ed.), *The Psychology of Learning and Motivation: Advances in Research and Theory*, New York: Academic Press.

Bandura, A. (1977) *Social Learning Theory*, New York: General Learning Press.

Barnes, C. (1991) *Disabled People in Britain and Discrimination: A Case for Anti-Discrimination Legislation*, London: Hurst & Co.

Bitsika, V. (2003) '"But I'm not really bad": using an ideographic versus a nomothetic approach to understand the reasons for difficult behaviour in children', *Journal of Psychologists and Counsellors in Schools*, 13(1): 87–98.

Bjork, E.L. and Bjork, R.A. (2011) 'Making things hard on yourself, but in a good way: creating desirable difficulties to enhance learning', in M.A. Gernsbacher, R.W. Pew, L.M. Hough and J.R. Pomerantz (eds), *Psychology and the Real World: Essays Illustrating Fundamental Contributions to Society*, New York: Worth Publishers.

Black, P. and Wiliam, D. (1998) 'Inside the black box: raising standards through classroom assessment', *Phi Delta Kappan*, 80(2): 139–48.

Black-Hawkins, K., Florian, L. and Rouse, M. (2007) *Achievement and Inclusion in Schools*, London: Routledge.

Bligh, C. (2014) *The Silent Experiences of Young Bilingual Learners*, Rotterdam: Sense Publishers.

Bloom, B.S. (1956) *Taxonomy of Educational Objectives Handbook 1: The Cognitive Domain*, New York: David McKay.

Boaler, J. (2013) 'Ability and mathematics: the mindset revolution that is reshaping education', *Forum*, 55(1): 143–52.

Bobis, J., Mulligan, J. and Lowrie, T. (2012) *Mathematics for Children: Challenging Children to Think Mathematically*, Sydney: Pearson Education.

Bowlby, J. (1988) *A Secure Base: Clinical Applications of Attachment Theory*, London: Routledge.

Braaksma, M.A.H., Rijlaarsdam, G. and van den Bergh, H. (2002) 'Observational learning and the effects of model-observer similarity', *Journal of Educational Psychology*, 94(2): 405–15.

Bronfenbrenner, U. (1992) 'Ecological systems theory', in R. Vasta (ed.), *Six Theories of Child Development: Revised Formulations and Current Issues*, London: Jessica Kingsley Publishers.

Brookhart, S.M. (2001) 'Successful students' formative and summative uses of assessment information', *Assessment in Education*, 8(2): 153–69.

Brown, G.D.A. and Deavers, R.P. (1999) 'Units of analysis in nonword reading: evidence from children and adults', *Journal of Experimental Child Psychology*, 73(3): 208–42.

Brown, K. (2018) *Bullying: A Review of the Evidence*, available at: https://epi.org.uk/publications-and-research/bullying-a-review-of-the-evidence/

Bruner, J.S. (1966) *Toward a Theory of Instruction*, Cambridge, MA: Belknap Press.

Bruner, J.S. (1978) 'The role of dialogue in language acquisition', in A. Sinclair, R.J. Jarvella and W.J.M. Levelt (eds), *The Child's Concept of Language*, New York: Springer.

Butler, R. (1987) 'Task-involving and ego-involving properties of evaluation: effects of different feedback conditions on motivational perceptions, interest, and performance', *Journal of Educational Psychology*, 79(4): 474–82.

Cambridge Assessment (2019) *Metacognition*, available at: www.cambridgeinternational.org/Images/272307-metacognition.pdf

Cantor, P., Osher, D., Berg, J., Steyer, L. and Rose, T. (2019) 'Malleability, plasticity, and individuality: how children learn and develop in context', *Applied Developmental Science*, 23(4): 307–37.

Carpenter, B., Ashdown, R. and Bovair, K. (eds) (2017) *Enabling Access: Effective Teaching and Learning for Pupils with Learning Difficulties* (2nd edn), London: Routledge.

Carter, A. (2015) *Carter Review of Initial Teacher Training (ITT)*, London: DfE.

Chodkiewicz, A.R. and Boyle, C. (2016) 'Promoting positive learning in students aged 10–12 years using attribution retraining and cognitive behavioural therapy: a pilot study', *School Psychology International*, 37(5): 519–35.

Chodkiewicz, A.R. and Boyle, C. (2017) 'Positive psychology school-based interventions: a reflection on current success and future directions', *Review of Education*, 5(1): 60–86.

Claro, S., Pauneskub, D. and Dweck, C.S. (2016) 'Growth mindset tempers the effects of poverty on academic achievement', *PNAS*, available at: https://web.stanford.edu/~paunesku/articles/claro_2016.pdf

Cobley, D. (2018) *Disability and International Development: A Guide for Students and Practitioners*, London: Routledge.

Coe, R., Aloisi, C., Higgins, S. and Major, L.E. (2014) *What Makes Great Teaching? Review of the Underpinning Research: Project Report*, London: Sutton Trust.

Cole, B. (2005) 'Good faith and effort? Perspectives on educational inclusion', *Disability and Society*, 20(3): 331–44.

Condie, R., Livingston, K. and Seagraves, L. (2005) *Evaluation of the Assessment for Learning Programme: Final Report*, Glasgow: Quality in Education Centre, University of Strathclyde.

Corbett, J. (1992) 'Careful teaching: researching a special career', *British Educational Research Journal*, 18(3): 235–43.

Corbett, J. (1999) 'Inclusive education and school culture', *International Journal of Inclusive Education*, 3(1): 53–61.

Corbett, J. (2001) 'Teaching approaches which support inclusive education: a connective pedagogy', *British Journal of Special Education*, 28(2): 55–9.

Cummins, J. (1980) 'Psychological assessment of immigrant children: logic or intuition?', *Journal of Multilingual and Multicultural Development*, 1(2): 97–111.

Darling-Hammond, L., Flook, L., Cook-Harvey, C., Barron, B. and Osher, D. (2019) 'Implications for educational practice of the science of learning and development', *Applied Developmental Science*, 24(2): 97–140.

Davies, J., Hallam, S. and Ireson, J. (2003) 'Ability groupings in the primary school: issues arising from practice', *Research Papers in Education*, 18(1): 45–60.

Day, C., Stobart, G., Sammons, P., Kington, A., Gu, Q., Smees, R. and Mujtaba, T. (2006) *Variations in Teachers' Work, Lives and Effectiveness*, London: DfES.

Denham, S.A., Bassett, H.H., Brown, C.A., Way, E. and Steed, J. (2015) '"I know how you feel": preschoolers' emotion knowledge contributes to early school success', *Journal of Early Childhood Research*, 13(3): 252–62.

Department for Education (DfE) (2011) *Teachers' Standards: Guidance for School Leaders, School Staff and Governing Bodies*, London: DfE.

Department for Education (DfE) (2016) *Behaviour and Discipline in Schools: Advice for Headteachers and School Staff*, London: DfE.

Department for Education (DfE) (2019a) *Early Career Framework*, London: DfE.

Department for Education (DfE) (2019b) *ITT Core Content Framework*, London: DfE.

Department for Education (DfE) and Department of Health (DoH) (2015) *Special Educational Needs and Disability Code of Practice*, London: DfE & DoH.

Dewsbury, G., Clarke, K., Randall, D., Rouncefield, M. and Sommerville, I. (2004) 'The antisocial model of disability', *Disability and Society*, 19(2): 145–58.

Diamond, A. (2013) 'Executive functions', *Annual Review of Psychology*, 64(1): 135–68.

Dixon, A. (2002) 'Editorial', *Forum*, 44(1): 1.

Dowling, M. (2010) *Young Children's Personal, Social and Emotional Development* (3rd edn), London: SAGE.

Dunne, L. (2009) 'Discourses of inclusion: a critique', *Power and Education*, 1(1): 42–56.

Durlak, J.A., Weissberg, R.P., Dymnicki, A.P., Taylor, R.D. and Schellinger, K.B. (2011) 'The impact of enhancing students' social and emotional learning: a meta-analysis of school-based universal interventions', *Child Development*, 82(1): 405–32.

Dweck, C.S. (1999) *Self-Theories: Their Role in Motivation, Personality, and Development*, Hove: Psychology Press.

Dweck, C.S. (2007) 'Boosting achievement with messages that motivate', *Education Canada*, 47(2): 6–10.

Dweck, C.S. (2008) *Mindset: The New Psychology of Success*, New York: Ballantine Books.

Dweck, C.S. (2009) 'Mindsets: developing talent through a growth mindset', *Olympic Coach*, 21(1): 4–7.

Dweck, C.S. (2010) 'Giving students meaningful work', *Educational Leadership*, 68(1): 16–20.

Dyson, A. (2001) 'Special needs education as the way to equity: an alternative approach?', *Support for Learning*, 16(3): 99–104.

Dyson, A., Farrell, P., Polat, F., Hutcheson, G. and Gallanaugh, F. (2004) *Inclusion and Pupil Achievement*, Nottingham: DfES.

Education Endowment Foundation (EEF) (2015) *Making the Best Use of Teaching Assistants: Guidance Report*, London: EEF.

Education Endowment Foundation (EEF) (2018) *Metacognition and Self-Regulated Learning*, London: EEF.

Education Endowment Foundation (EEF) (2019) *Improving Behaviour in Schools*, London: EEF.

Ellis, S. and Tod, J. (2018) *Behaviour for Learning: Promoting Positive Relationships in the Class-room*, London: Routledge.

Erten, O. and Savage, R.S. (2012) 'Moving forward in inclusive education research', *International Journal of Inclusive Education*, 16(2): 221–33.

Farrell, P. (2001) 'Special education in the last twenty years: have things really got better?', *British Journal of Special Education*, 28(1): 3–9.

Farrington, C.A., Roderick, M., Allensworth, E., Nagaoka, J., Keyes, T.S., Johnson, D.W. and Beechum, N.O. (2012) *Teaching Adolescents to Become Learners: The Role of Noncognitive Factors in Shaping School Performance – A Critical Literature Review*, Chicago, IL: University of Chicago Consortium on Chicago School Research.

Flórez, M.T. and Sammons, P. (2013) *Assessment for Learning: Effects and Impact*, Berkshire: CfBT Education Trust.

Florian, L. (2009) 'Towards inclusive pedagogy', in P. Hick, R. Kershner and P. Farrell (eds), *Psychology for Inclusive Education*, London: Routledge.

Florian, L. and Beaton, M. (2018) 'Inclusive pedagogy in action: getting it right for every child', *International Journal of Inclusive Education*, 22(8): 870–84.

Florian, L., Black-Hawkins, K. and Rouse, M. (2017) *Achievement and Inclusion in Schools* (2nd edn), London: Routledge.

Forlin, C. and Chambers, D. (2011) 'Teacher preparation for inclusive education: increasing knowledge but raising concerns', *Asia-Pacific Journal of Teacher Education*, 39(1): 17–32.

Foucault, M. (1975) *Abnormal Lectures at the Collège de France 1974–75*, in L.J. Graham (2006), 'Caught in the net: a Foucaultian interrogation of the incidental effects of limited notions of inclusion', *International Journal of Inclusive Education*, 10(1): 3–25.

Foucault, M. (1977) *Discipline and Punish: The Birth of the Prison*, Harmondsworth: Penguin.

Foucault, M. (1984) 'Docile bodies', in P. Rabinow (ed.), *The Foucault Reader*, New York: Pantheon Books.

Fullan, M. (2007) *The New Meaning of Educational Change* (4th edn), New York: Teachers College Press.

Gabel, S.L. (2010) 'Foreword: disability and equity in education and special education', in A. Azzopardi (ed.), *Making Sense of Inclusive Education: Where Everyone Belongs*, Saarbrücken: VDM Verlag Dr. Müller.

Gayton, S. and Lovell, G. (2012) 'Resilience in ambulance service paramedics and its relationships with well-being and general health', *Traumatology*, 18(1): 58–64.

Georghiades, P. (2004) 'From the general to the situated: three decades of metacognition', *International Journal of Science Education*, 26(3): 365–83.

Gerhardt, S. (2014) *Why Love Matters: How Affection Shapes a Baby's Brain*, London: Routledge.

Gipps, C., McCallum, B., Hargreaves, E. and Pickering, A. (2005) *From TA to Assessment for Learning: The Impact of Assessment Policy on Teachers' Assessment Practice*, paper presented at the British Educational Research Association Annual Conference, University of Glamorgan, 14–17 September.

Glazzard, J. (2011) 'Perceptions of the barriers to inclusion in one primary school: voices of teachers and teaching assistants', *Support for Learning: British Journal of Learning Support*, 26(2): 56–63.

Glazzard, J. (2017) 'Assessing reading development through systematic synthetic phonics', *English in Education*, 51(1): 44–57.

Goodley, D. (2007) 'Towards socially just pedagogies: Deleuzoguattarian critical disability studies', *International Journal of Inclusive Education*, 11(3): 317–34.

Goodley, D. and Runswick-Cole, K. (2010) 'Len Barton, inclusion and critical disability studies: theorizing disabled childhoods', *International Studies in Sociology of Education*, 20(4): 273–90.

Goodman, A., Joshi, H., Nasim, B. and Tyler, C. (2015) *Social and Emotional Skills in Childhood and Their Long-Term Effects on Adult Life: A Review for the Early Intervention Foundation*, London: Institute of Education/UCL.

Goswami, U. (2005) 'Synthetic phonics and learning to read: a cross-language perspective', *Educational Psychology in Practice*, 21(4): 273–82.

Goswami, U. and Bryant, P. (2007) *Children's Cognitive Development and Learning*, Cambridge: University of Cambridge Faculty of Education.

Goswami, U., Ziegler, J.C., Dalton, L. and Schneider, W. (2003) 'Non-word reading across orthographies: how flexible is the choice of reading units?', *Applied Psycholinguistics*, 24(1): 235–47.

Gough, P.B. and Tunmer, W.E. (1986) 'Decoding, reading and reading disability', *Remedial and Special Education*, 7(1): 6–10.

Graham, L.J. (2006), 'Caught in the net: a Foucaultian interrogation of the incidental effects of limited notions of inclusion', *International Journal of Inclusive Education*, 10(1): 3–25.

Graham, L.J. and Harwood, V. (2011) 'Developing capabilities for social inclusion: engaging diversity through inclusive school communities', *International Journal of Inclusive Education*, 15(1): 135–52.

Graham, L.J. and Scott, W. (2016) *Teacher Preparation for Inclusive Education: Initial Teacher Education and In-Service Professional Development*, available at: www.deafeducation.vic.edu.au/Documents/NewsEvents/LitRevIncTe.pdf

Graham, L.J. and Slee, R. (2008) 'An illusory interiority: interrogating the discourse/s of inclusion', *Educational Philosophy and Theory*, 40(2): 247–60.

Graham, S. and Harris, K.R. (1994) 'The role and development of self-regulation in the writing process', in D.H. Schunk and B.J. Zimmerman (eds), *Self-Regulation of Learning and Performance: Issues and Educational Applications*, Hillsdale, NJ: Erlbaum.

Gutman, L.M. and Schoon, I. (2013) *The Impact of Non-Cognitive Skills on Outcomes for Young People*, London: EEF.

Handelsman, J., Ebert-May, D., Beichner, R., Bruns, P., Chang, A., De Haan, R., et al. (2004) 'Scientific teaching', *Science*, 23(304): 521–2.

Hansen, J.H. (2012) 'Limits to inclusion', *International Journal of Inclusive Education*, 16(1): 89–98.

Hattie, J. and Donoghue, G. (2016) 'Learning strategies: a synthesis and conceptual model', *npj Science of Learning*, 1(16013), https://doi.org/10.1038/npjscilearn.2016.13

Hattie, J. and Timperley, H. (2007) 'The power of feedback', *Review of Educational Research*, 77(1): 81–112.

Hayward, L. and Spencer, E. (2010) 'The complexities of change: formative assessment in Scotland', *Curriculum Journal*, 21(2): 161–77.

Hegarty, S. (2001) 'Inclusive education: a case to answer', *Journal of Moral Education*, 30(3): 243–9.

Hehir, T., Grindal, T., Freeman, B., Lamoreau, R., Borquaye, Y. and Burke, S. (2016) *A Summary of the Evidence on Inclusive Education*, available at: https://alana.org.br/wpcontent/uploads/2016/12/A_Summary_of_the_evidence_on_inclusive_education.pdf

Higgins, S., Katsipataki, M., Kokotsaki, D., Coleman, R., Major, L.E. and Coe, R. (2014) *The Sutton Trust: Education Endowment Foundation Teaching and Learning Toolkit*, London: EEF.

HM Government (2006) *Education and Inspections Act 2006*, available at: www.educationengland.org.uk/documents/acts/2006-education-and-inspections-act.html

HM Government (2010) *Equality Act 2010*, available at: www.legislation.gov.uk/ukpga/2010/15/part/2/chapter/1

Hodkinson, A. (2012) '"All present and correct?" Exclusionary inclusion within the English education system', *Disability and Society*, 27(5): 675–88.

Hodkinson, A. and Vickerman, P. (2009) *Key Issues in Special Educational Needs and Inclusion*, London: SAGE.

International Bureau of Education (IBE-UNESCO) (2016) *Training Tools for Curriculum Development: Reaching Out to All Learners – A Resource Pack for Supporting Inclusive Education*, available at: http://unesdoc.unesco.org/images/0024/002432/243279e.pdf

Jindal-Snape, D. and Miller, D. (2010) 'Understanding transitions through self-esteem and resilience', in D. Jindal-Snape (ed.), *Educational Transitions: Moving Stories from Around the World*, London: Routledge.

Johnson, D.W., Johnson, R.T. and Stanne, M.E. (2000) *Cooperative Learning Methods: A Meta-Analysis*, available at: www.semanticscholar.org/paper/Cooperative-learning-methods%3A-A-meta-analysis.-Johnson-Johnson/93e997fd0e883cf7cceb3b1b612096c27aa40f90

Johnson, R. and Watson, J. (2004) 'Accelerating the development of reading, spelling and phonemic awareness', *Reading and Writing*, 17(3): 327–57.

Kellard, K., Costello, M., Godfrey, D., Griffiths, E. and Rees, C. (2008) *Evaluation of the Developing Thinking and Assessment for Learning Development Programme*, Cardiff: Welsh Assembly Government.

Kirschner, P.A., Sweller, J. and Clark, R. (2006) 'Why minimal guidance during instruction does not work: an analysis of the failure of constructivist, discovery, problem-based, experiential, and inquiry-based teaching', *Educational Psychologist*, 41(2): 75–86.

Kirton, A., Hallam, S., Peffers, J., Robertson, P. and Stobart, G. (2007) 'Revolution, evolution or a Trojan Horse? Piloting assessment for learning in some Scottish primary schools', *British Educational Research Journal*, 33(4): 605–27.

Kuroda, K., Kartika, D. and Kitamura, Y. (2017) *Implications for Teacher Training and Support for Inclusive Education in Cambodia: An Empirical Case Study in a Developing Country*, JICA Research Institute Working Paper 148, available at: www.jica.go.jp/jica-ri/publication/workingpaper/wp_148.html

Landerl, K. (2000) 'Influences of orthographic consistency and reading instruction on the development of nonword reading skills', *European Journal of Psychology of Education*, 15(3): 239–57.

Lloyd, C. (2008) 'Removing barriers to achievement: a strategy for inclusion or exclusion?', *International Journal of Inclusive Education*, 12(2): 221–36.

Luthar, S.S. (2006) 'Resilience in development: a synthesis of research across five decades', in D. Cicchetti and D.J. Cohen (eds), *Development Psychopathology: Risk, Disorder and Adaptation*, Hoboken, NJ: Wiley.

MacPhail, A. and Halbert, J. (2010) '"We had to do intelligent thinking during recent PE": students' and teachers' experiences of assessment for learning in post-primary physical education', *Assessment in Education: Principles, Policy and Practice*, 17(1): 23–39.

Maguire, E.A., Woollett, K. and Spiers, H.J. (2006) 'London taxi drivers and bus drivers: a structural MRI and neuropsychological analysis', *Hippocampus*, 16(12): 1091–101.

Masten, A. and Garmezy, N. (1985) 'Risk, vulnerability, and protective factors in developmental psychopathology', in B.B. Lahey and A.E. Kazdin (eds), *Advances in Clinical Child Psychology*, New York: Plenum Press.

McDermott, P.A., Mordell, M. and Stoltzfus, J.C. (2001) 'The organization of student performance in American schools: discipline, motivation, verbal learning, nonverbal learning', *Journal of Educational Psychology*, 93(1): 65–76.

McLeod, S. (2013) 'Stages of memory: encoding storage and retrieval', *Simply Psychology*, available at: www.simplypsychology.org/memory.html

Miller, G. (1956) 'The magical number seven, plus or minus two: some limits on our capacity for processing information', *The Psychological Review*, 63(2): 81–97.

Mittler, P. (2000) *Working Towards Inclusive Education: Social Contexts*, London: David Fulton.

Moore, D.S. (2015) *The Developing Genome: An introduction to Behavioral Epigenetics*, New York: Oxford University Press.

Mruk, C. (1999) *Self-Esteem: Research, Theory and Practice*, London: Free Association Books.

Nelson, L.L. (2014) *Design and Deliver: Planning and Teaching Using Universal Design for Learning*, Baltimore, MD: Brookes.

Nilholm, C. (2006) 'Special education, inclusion and democracy', *European Journal of Special Needs Education*, 21(4): 431–45.

Nind, M. (2005) 'Inclusive education: discourse and action', *British Educational Research Journal*, 31(2): 269–75.

Nind, M., Rix, J., Sheehy, K. and Simmons, K. (2003) *Inclusive Education: Diverse Perspectives*, London: David Fulton.

Office for Standards in Education (Ofsted) (2017) *Bold Beginnings: The Reception Curriculum in a Sample of Good and Outstanding Primary Schools*, Manchester: Ofsted.

Office for Standards in Education (Ofsted) (2019) *Education Inspection Framework*, Manchester: Ofsted.

Oliver, M. (1990) *The Politics of Disablement*, Basingstoke: Macmillan.

Oliver, M. (1996) *Understanding Disability*, Basingstoke: Macmillan.

Ollerton, M. (2001) 'Inclusion, learning and teaching mathematics: beliefs and values', in P. Gates (ed.), *Issues in Mathematics Teaching*, London: RoutledgeFalmer.

Organisation for Economic Co-operation and Development (OECD) (2015) *Skills for Social Progress: The Power of Social and Emotional Skills*, Paris: OECD.

Paas, F., Renkl, A. and Sweller, J. (2003) 'Cognitive load theory: instructional implications of the interaction between information structures and cognitive architecture', *Instructional Science*, 32(1/2): 1–8.

Pather, S. (2007) 'Demystifying inclusion: implications for sustainable inclusive practice', *International Journal of Inclusive Education*, 11(5/6): 627–43.

Pavlov, I.P. (1927) *Conditioned Reflexes: An Investigation of the Physiological Activity of the Cerebral Cortex*, Oxford: Oxford University Press.

Philpott, C. and Poultney, V. (2018) *Evidence-Based Teaching: A Critical Overview for Enquiring Teachers*, St Albans: Critical Publishing.

Piaget, J. (1936) *Origins of Intelligence in the Child*, London: Routledge & Kegan Paul.

Piaget, J. and Cook, M.T. (1952) *The Origins of Intelligence in Children*, New York: International University Press.

Pizzuto, S.A. (2010) 'A teacher, a classroom, a school: a holistic approach towards inclusion', in A. Azzopardi (ed.), *Making Sense of Inclusive Education: Where Everyone Belongs*, Saarbrücken: VDM Verlag Dr. Müller.

Rawson, A. and Kintsch, W. (2005) 'Rereading effects depend on time of test', *Journal of Educational Psychology*, 97(1): 70–80.

Reyes, A.T., Andrusyszyn, M.A., Iwaaiw, C., Forchuk, C. and Babenko-Mould, Y. (2015) 'Resilience in nursing education: an integrative review', *Journal of Nursing Education*, 54(8): 438–44.

Rhim, L.M. and Lancet, S. (2018) *How Personalized Learning Models Can Meet the Needs of Students with Disabilities: Thrive Public Schools Case Study*, available at: www.crpe.org/publications/personalized-learning-models-meet-needs-students-disabilities-thrive-case-study

Roaf, C. (1988) 'The concept of a whole school approach to special needs', in O. Robinson and G. Thomas (eds), *Tackling Learning Difficulties*, London: Hodder & Stoughton.

Roaf, C. and Bines, H. (1989) 'Needs, rights and opportunities in special education', in C. Roaf and H. Bines (eds), *Needs, Rights and Opportunities: Developing Approaches to Special Education*, London: Falmer.

Roffey, S. (2017) 'Ordinary magic needs ordinary magicians: the power and practice of positive relationships for building youth resilience and wellbeing', *Kognition & Pædagogik*, 103: 38–57.

Rose, J. (2006) *Independent Review of the Teaching of Early Reading*, London: DfES.

Rose, R. and Doveston, M. (2015) 'Collaboration across cultures: planning and delivering professional development for inclusive education in India', *Support for Learning*, 30(3): 177–91.

Sæbønes, A.-M., Bieler, R.B., Baboo, N., Banham, L., Singal, N., Howgego, C., et al. (2015) *Towards a Disability Inclusive Education: Background Paper for the Oslo Summit on Education for Development*, available at: www.usaid.gov/sites/default/files/documents/1865/Oslo_Ed_Summit_DisabilityInclusive_Ed.pdf

Sailor, W. (2015) 'Advances in schoolwide inclusive school reform', *Remedial and Special Education*, 36(2): 94–9.

Sammons, P., Lindorff, A.M., Ortega, L. and Kington, A. (2016) 'Inspiring teaching: learning from exemplary practitioners', *Journal of Professional Capital and Community*, 1(2): 124–44.

Sanderson, B. and Brewer, M. (2017) 'What do we know about student resilience in health professional education? A scoping review of the literature', *Nurse Education Today*, 58: 65–71.

Schuelka, M.J. and Johnstone, C.J. (2012) 'Global trends in meeting the educational rights of children with disabilities: from international institutions to local responses', *Reconsidering Development*, 2(2), available at: https://pubs.lib.umn.edu/index.php/reconsidering/article/view/573

Schunk, D.H., Hanson, A.R. and Cox, P.D. (1987) 'Peer-model attributes and children's achievement behaviors', *Journal of Educational Psychology*, 79(1): 54–61.

Seymour, P.H.K., Aro, M. and Erskine, J.M. (2003) 'Foundation literacy acquisition in European orthographies', *British Journal of Psychology*, 94(2): 143–74.

Sharma, U., Simi, J. and Forlin, C. (2015) 'Preparedness of pre-service teachers for inclusive education in the Solomon Islands', *Australian Journal of Teacher Education*, 40(5): 103–16.

Shogren, K.A., McCart, A.B., Lyon, K.J. and Sailor, W.S. (2015) 'All means all: building knowledge for inclusive schoolwide transformation', *Research and Practice for Persons with Severe Disabilities*, 40(3): 173–91.

Sikes, P. (1997) *Parents Who Teach: Stories from Home and from School*, London: Cassell.

Sikes, P., Lawson, H. and Parker, M. (2007) 'Voices on: teachers and teaching assistants talk about inclusion', *International Journal of Inclusive Education*, 11(3): 355–70.

Skidmore, D. (2004) *Inclusion: The Dynamic of School Development*, Berkshire: Open University Press.

Skinner, B.F. (1938) *The Behaviour of Organisms: An Experimental Analysis*, New York: Appleton-Century.

Skrtic, T.M. (1991) 'Students with special educational needs: artefacts of the traditional curriculum', in M. Ainscow (ed.), *Effective Schools for All*, London: David Fulton.

Slavich, G.M. and Cole, S.W. (2013) 'The emerging field of human social genomics', *Clinical Psychological Science*, 1(3): 331–48.

Slee, R. (2001a) 'Social justice and the changing directions in educational research: the case of inclusive education', *International Journal of Inclusive Education*, 5(2/3): 167–77.

Slee, R. (2001b) 'Inclusion in practice: does practice make perfect?', *Educational Review*, 53(2): 113–23.

Slee, R. (2011) *The Irregular School: Exclusion, Schooling and Inclusive Education*, London: Routledge.

Slee, R. and Allan, J. (2001) 'Excluding the included: a reconsideration of inclusive education', *International Studies in Sociology of Education*, 11(2): 173–91.

Snowling, M.J., Hulme, C., Bailey A.M., Stothard, S.E. and Lindsay, G. (2011) *Better Communication Research Programme: Language and Literacy Attainment of Pupils During Early Years and Through KS2 – Does Teacher Assessment at Five Provide a Valid Measure of Children's Current and Future Educational Attainments?* London: DfE.

Spencer, L.H. and Hanley, J.R. (2003) 'Effects of orthographic transparency on reading and phoneme awareness in children learning to read in Wales', *British Journal of Psychology*, 94(1): 1–28.

Stallman, H.M. (2011) 'Embedding resilience within the tertiary curriculum: a feasibility study', *Higher Education Research and Development*, 30(2): 121–33.

Stephens, D. (2013) 'Teaching professional sexual ethics across the seminary curriculum', *Religious Education*, 108(2): 193–209.

Sternberg, R. (2005) 'Intelligence, competence, and expertise', in A. Elliot and C.S. Dweck (eds), *The Handbook of Competence and Motivation*, New York: Guilford Press.

Stets, J.E. and Burke, P.J. (2014) 'Self-esteem and Identities', *Sociological Perspectives*, 57(4): 409–33.

Stiggins, R. and Arter, J. (2002) *Assessment for Learning: International Perspectives*, Proceedings of an International Conference, Chester, 18 September.

Stuart, M. (2006) 'Teaching reading: why start with systematic phonics teaching?', *The Psychology of Education Review*, 30(2): 6–17.

Subban, P. and Mahlo, D. (2017) '"My attitude, my responsibility": investigating the attitudes and intentions of pre-service teachers toward inclusive education between teacher preparation cohorts in Melbourne and Pretoria', *International Journal of Inclusive Education*, 21(4): 441–61.

Swain, J. and French, S. (2003) 'Towards an affirmation model of disability', in M. Nind, J. Rix, K. Sheehy and K. Simmons (eds), *Inclusive Education: Diverse Perspectives*, London: David Fulton.

Sylva, K., Melhuish, E., Sammons, P., Siraj-Blatchford, I. and Taggart, B. (2004) *The Effective Provision of Pre-School Education (EPPE) Project: Findings from Pre-School to End of Key Stage 1*, London: Institute of Education/UCL.

Tafarodi, R.W. and Milne, A.B. (2002) 'Decomposing global self-esteem', *Journal of Personality*, 70(4): 443–83.

Tafarodi, R.W. and Swann, W.B. (1995) 'Self-liking and self-competence as dimensions of global self-esteem: initial validation of a measure', *Journal of Personality Assessment*, 65(2): 322–42.

Thomas, G. and Loxley, A. (2007) *Deconstructing Special Education and Constructing Inclusion* (2nd edn), Berkshire: Open University Press.

Thompson, R.A. and Lagattuta, K. (2006) 'Feeling and understanding: early emotional development', in K. McCartney and D. Phillips (eds), *The Blackwell Handbook of Early Childhood Development*, Oxford: Blackwell.

Tomlinson, S. (1985) 'The expansion of special education', *Oxford Review of Education*, 11(2): 157–65.

Torgerson, C.J., Brooks, G. and Hall, J. (2006) *A Systematic Review of the Research Literature on the Use of Phonics in the Teaching of Reading and Spelling*, London: DfES.

Torrance, H. and Pryor, J. (2001) 'Developing formative assessment in the classroom: using action research to explore and modify theory', *British Educational Research Journal*, 27(5): 615–31.

Training and Development Agency for Schools (TDA) (2007) *Developing Trainees' Subject Knowledge for Teaching*, London: TDA.

Tregaskis, C. (2002) 'Social model theory: the story so far', *Disability and Society*, 17(4): 457–70.

Trundley, R., Wreghitt, C., Edginton, H., Eversett, H. and Burke, S. (2017) *Supporting Children to Be Active and Influential Participants in Mathematics Lessons Through Effective Use of Assigning Competence and Pre-Teaching*, Exeter: Babcock LDP.

United Nations (UN) (2016) *General Comment No. 4 – Article 24: Right to Inclusive Education*, CRPD/C/GC/4, available at: www.ohchr.org/en/hrbodies/crpd/pages/gc.aspx

Villa, R.A. and Thousand, J.S. (2016) *Leading an Inclusive School: Access and Success for All Students*, Alexandria, VA: ASCD.

Vygotsky, L.S. (1978) *Mind in Society: The Development of Higher Psychological Processes*, Cambridge, MA: Harvard University Press.

Walton, P.D., Bowden, M.E., Kurtz, S.L. and Angus, M. (2001) 'Evaluation of a rime-based reading program with Shuswap and Heiltsuk First Nations prereaders', *Reading and Writing*, 14(3): 229–64.

Webb, M. and Jones, J. (2009) 'Exploring tensions in developing assessment for learning', *Assessment in Education*, 16(2): 165–84.

Weisberg, D., Hirsh-Pasek, K. and Golinkoff, R. (2013) 'Guided play: where curricular goals meet a playful pedagogy', *Mind, Brain and Education*, 7(2), https://doi.org/10.1111/mbe.12015

Wilson, J. (1999) 'Some conceptual difficulties about inclusion', *Support for Learning*, 14(3): 110–12.

Wilson, J. (2000) 'Doing justice to inclusion', *European Journal of Special Needs Education*, 15(3): 297–304.

Winch, C., Oancea, A. and Orchard, J. (2015) 'The contribution of educational research to teachers' professional learning: philosophical understandings', *Oxford Review of Education*, 41(2): 202–16.

World Health Organization (WHO) (2001) *Towards a Common Language for Functioning, Disability and Health*, Geneva: WHO.

Wyse, D. and Goswami, U. (2008) 'Synthetic phonics and the teaching of reading', *British Educational Research Journal*, 34(6): 691–710.

Wyse, D. and Styles, M. (2007) 'Synthetic phonics and the teaching of reading: the debate surrounding England's "Rose Report"', *Literacy*, 41(1): 35–42.

Zimmerman, B.J. (2010) 'Becoming a self-regulated learner: an overview', *Theory into Practice*, 41(2): 64–70.

We want to

EMPOWER TEACHERS

TO BE
RESEARCHERS,

RATHER THAN ADOPTING A MODEL IN
WHICH PROFESSIONAL RESEARCHERS
DETERMINE THE PRACTICES OF TEACHERS.

INSTEAD, WE BELIEVE THAT THE
PRACTICES OF TEACHERS SHOULD INFORM
THE BODY OF RESEARCH, RATHER THAN
THE OTHER WAY AROUND.

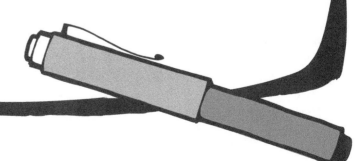

INDEX

ability groupings 21
Abiola, O.O. 21
able pupils 70
abstract concepts 16, 38–39, 49
active learning 2, 16, 40
adverse childhood experiences (ACEs) 87
adversity 7, 19, 31, 87
affirmative model of disability 64–66
Ainscow, M. 58
Alexander, R.J. 103
Allan, J. 58, 59, 60, 61
antisocial behaviours 18
Armstrong, D. 60, 61, 62
art and design 54
Arter, J. 80
assessment for learning 40, 74–84
Assessment Reform Group 76
assimilation 33, 58, 59, 61
authenticity 19
Avramidis, E. 58
Azzopardi, A. 58, 59

Baddeley, A.D. 26, 28
Bandura, A. 7, 48
Barnes, C. 63
basic interpersonal communication skills (BICS)
    71–72
Beaton, M. 70
behaviour 1, 7, 18, 85–95
behaviourist approaches to learning 13
bilingualism 71–72
Bines, H. 64
bioecological model of child development 11–12
biopsychosocial model of health 66–67
Bitsika, V. 88
Bjork, E.L. 25
Bjork, R.A. 25
Black, P. 74
Black-Hawkins, K. 59
Bligh, C. 71
Bloom's taxonomy 78–79
Boaler, J. 21
Bobis, J. 70
Bobo doll experiment 48
Bold Beginnings (Ofsted, 2017) 3
boundaries 7, 88
Bowlby, J. 6
Boyle, C. 87
Braaksma, M.A.H. 46

brain development 12, 21–22
brain plasticity 12, 21
Brewer, M. 19
Bronfenbrenner, U. 11–12
Brookhart, S.M. 80
Brown, K. 42, 87
Bruner, J. 15, 49
Bryant, P. 2
bullying 87
Burke, Jan 19
Butler, R. 82

Cantor, P. 12, 99
'careful teaching' 60
Carpenter, B. 68
Carter Review ix, 105
challenging behaviour 93
Chambers, D. 68
Chartered College of Teaching ix
child development 11, 12–16
child-initiated play 1, 3–4
Chodkiewicz, A.R. 87
chunking 31
Claro, S. 21
Cobley, D. 58
Coe, R. 25, 36, 89
cognitive academic language proficiency (CALP)
    71–72
cognitive development 2, 10, 13–15, 16
cognitive dissonance 33
cognitive load 29, 31–33
cognitive overload 29
Cole, B. 58, 60, 61
Cole, S.W. 12
collaborative learning 17, 96
common underlying proficiency (CUP) 71–72
communication and language development 2, 3, 71
communities of teachers 41
computing 55
concentration 10
Condie, R. 78
conditioned behaviours 13
conflict resolution 6; see also diffusing situations
conservation task 14
consolidation, offering opportunities for 69
constructivist approaches to learning 13–15,
    22–23, 33
continuing professional development (CPD) 41,
    45, 67

Cook, M.T. 33
coping models 46–47
Corbett, J. 58
Cummins, J. 71
curriculum planning 25, 68

Darling-Hammond, L. 10, 17, 31
Davies, J. 21
Day, C. 86
Deavers, R.P. 42
deduction skills 44
deficit-based views of difference 59, 60, 61
Denham, S.A. 6
Department for Education (DfE) 8, 11, 25, 37, 47,
     57, 75, 86, 91, 97
design and technology 54
Dewsbury, G. 63
Dhindsa, H.S. 21
dialogue 17, 103
Diamond, A. 2
differentiated instruction 10, 70, 102
difficulty, adding in deliberate 102
diffusing situations 92
dignity 58, 60
disability, models of 62–67
discipline 1, 85–95; see also behaviour
diversity 56–73
Dixon, A. 21
Donoghue, G. 69
Doveston, M. 67
Dowling, M. 6
drama 23, 40
Dunne, L. 62
Durlak, J.A. 6
Dweck, C.S. 21, 91
dyslexia 43
Dyson, A. 58, 61

early years 1–9
ecological perspectives 58
Education Endowment Foundation (EEF) ix, 69,
     70, 85, 91, 96, 99
egocentricity 15
Ellis, S. 88
emotional and social contexts for learning 10
emotional development 6
English 52, 100
English as an Additional Language (EAL) 71–72
environmental factors 4, 10, 11, 12, 13, 16, 58, 87
episodic buffer 26–27, 28–29
episodic memory 29
Equality Act 2010 57
Erten, O. 57, 58
evaluating learning 100–101
executive functioning skills 2, 6
experiences, learning through 12, 16, 17, 40; see
     also play-based learning
explanations 51

Farrell, P. 57, 60
Farrington, C.A. 98
feedback 77, 81–82, 89
fixed mindsets 21
Flórez, M.T. 76, 77, 80, 82
Florian, L. 56, 58, 59, 62, 70
Forlin, C. 68
formative assessment 74–84
Foucault, M. 61
foundation stage 2–3
French, S. 64–65
Fullan, M. 67

Gabel, S.L. 58
Garmezy, N. 19
Gayton, S. 19
genetics 12
geography 53
Georghiades, P. 98
Gerhardt, S. 6
Gipps, C. 78, 80
Glazzard, J. 42, 59
Goodley, D. 61
Goodman, A. 2
Goswami, U. 2, 42
Gough, P.B. 42
Graham, L.J. 46, 58, 59, 61, 62, 68
grapheme–phoneme correspondences
     (GPCs) 42, 44
graphic organisers 100
group work 17, 40, 96
growth mindsets 21–22, 91
guided learning 102
guided play 1
Gutman, L.M. 6

Halbert, J. 78, 82
Handelsman, J. 33
Hanley, J.R. 42
Hansen, J.H. 60
Harris, K.R. 46
Harwood, V. 58
Hattie, J. 69, 81
Hayward, L. 74
Hegarty, S. 60
Hehir, T. 58
Higgins, S. 96
higher-order thinking 8–9, 14, 69, 70, 78–79
history 53
Hitch, G.J. 26
Hodkinson, A. 59
'hooks,' lesson 40
humanitarian values 60, 61

iconic representation 15–16
inclusion 56–73
individual learner differences 58; see also
     differentiated instruction

inference skills 44
information processing 29–31
inhibitory control 2
initial teacher training 67
in-service professional development 67
inspection framework 75
Institute for Effective Education (IEE) ix
interest, fostering pupils' 40
interventions: deployment of TAs 69–70;
    English as an Additional Language (EAL)
    71–72; reading 43–44; social and emotional
    regulation 6

Jindal-Snape, D. 17, 18
Johnson, D.W. 17, 41
Johnstone, C.J. 58
Jones, J. 74, 78

Kellard, K. 78
Kintsch, W. 25
Kirschner, P.A. 25
Kirton, A. 78
Kuroda, K. 67

Lancet, S. 68
Landerl, K. 42
language/communication development 2, 3,
    43–44, 71
Latattuta, K. 6
leadership 68
learned helplessness 21
learning, theories of 10–24
learning behaviours 88–89
learning outcomes 68
learning talk 103
literacy 2, 3, 36, 41
Lloyd, C. 60, 61
long-term memory 25, 26, 29, 31–33
Lovell, G. 19
Loxley, A. 59, 61, 62, 67
Luthar, S.S. 19

MacPhail, A. 78, 82
Maguire, E.A. 21
Mahlo, D. 68
manipulative resources 39, 71
marking 80–81
Masten, A. 19
mastery models 46–47
mathematics 3, 37, 38–39, 47, 52–53, 100
McDermott, P.A. 88
McLeod, S. 26, 30
medical model of disability 62–63
memory 25–35, 48
mental health 67
metacognitive skills 17, 50, 96–104

Miller, D. 17, 18
Milne, A.B. 17
misconceptions, addressing 40, 44, 77, 78, 79–80
Mittler, P. 57, 58, 60
modelling 1, 6, 41, 46–55, 98, 99, 101–102
monitoring learning 100
Moore, D.S. 12
motivations for learning 48, 99
motor skills 3
Mruk, C. 17, 18
multisensory learning 2, 34, 51
music 54

National Foundation for Educational Research
    (NFER) ix
'needs' 59, 61–62, 64
negative reinforcement 90
Nelson, L.L. 68
neoliberalism 59, 61
neural pathways 2, 10, 12
neuroscience 2
Nilholm, C. 60
Nind, M. 57, 58, 60
number 3

Ofsted 75
Oliver, M. 63
Ollerton, M. 21
open-ended questioning 1, 3, 78
oracy, through all subjects 40
overlearning 34

Paas, F. 31
paired work 17, 40
Pather, S. 59
Pavlov, Ivan 13
PE (physical education) 54
peer assessment 77, 80
pencil grip 3
personal, social and emotional
    development 4–6, 87
personalised learning 68, 73
Philpott, C. 105
phonics 3, 34, 37, 41–42, 44
phonological loop 26–29
Piaget, Jean 13–15, 16, 33
Pizzuto, S.A. 60
planning, curriculum 25, 68
planning learning 76, 82, 100
plasticity, brain 12, 21
play-based learning 1, 2, 3–4, 44
positive reinforcement 90
positive sense of self 2
Poultney, V. 105
practice-informed research 105
praise 89–90

pre-teaching 69, 71
prior learning 69, 77, 102
procedural memory 29
professional development 41, 45, 67
progression knowledge 38
protected characteristics 57
Pryor, J. 78
punishment 90

quality first teaching 68, 73
questioning 51, 77–80

Rawson, A. 25
reading 3, 42–44; *see also* phonics
reasonable force 91–92
recapping prior learning 69, 77
reflective learning 101
reflective teaching practice 60
relationships 4–6, 12, 86–87
repetition of content 25, 26, 28
resilience 19–20
rewards/sanctions 13, 48, 90–91
Reyes, A.T. 19
Rhim, L.M. 68
rights 58, 59, 64
Roaf, C. 59, 64
Roffey, S. 6–7, 19, 87
Rose, J. 41, 42
Rose, R. 67
rules and routines 89
Runswick-Cole, K. 61

Sæbønes, A.-M. 68
Sailor, W. 68
Sammons, P. 76, 77, 80, 82, 87
sanctions/rewards 13, 48, 90–91
Sanderson, B. 19
Savage, R.S. 57, 58
scaffolding 17, 44, 49–50, 102–103
schemas 31–33
school leadership 68
schoolification of early years 2–3
Schoon, I. 6
Schuelka, M.J. 58
science 53
Scott, W. 68
self-assessment 77, 80, 100
self-competence 17–18
self-efficacy 19
self-esteem 17–19, 82
self-regulation 96, 98, 99
semantic memory 29, 30
SEND (special educational needs and disabilities) 56–73
sequencing 31, 69
Seymour, P.H.K. 42

Sharma, U. 68
Shogren, K.A. 68
Sikes, P. 58, 59, 60
simple view of reading (SVOR) 42–44
Skidmore, D. 61, 62
Skinner, D. 90
Skrtic, T.M. 61
Slavich, G.M. 12
Slee, R. 59, 60, 61, 62
Snowling, M.J. 2
social and emotional regulation 2, 4–7, 87
social constructivist approaches to learning 17, 22–23, 49
social contexts for learning 10
social justice 58, 59, 60
social learning theory 7, 48
social model of disability 63–64
special schools/units 58
spelling 41, 42
Spencer, E. 74
Spencer, L.H. 42
Stallman, H.M. 19
Stephens, D. 19
Sternberg, R. 21
Stets, Jan 19
Stiggins, R. 80
strategic learners 50
stress 10, 87
structured reflection 101
Stuart, M. 42
Styles, M. 42
Subban, P. 68
subject knowledge 25, 31, 33, 35, 36–45
success criteria 101
sustained shared thinking 1, 8–9
Swain, J. 64–65
Swann, W.B. 17
Sylva, K. 1, 3, 6, 8–9
symbolic representation 15–16
systematic synthetic phonics 3, 37, 41–42, 44

tabula rasa 13
Tafarodi, R.W. 17
talking through conflict 6
taxonomy of thinking skills 78
teaching assistants (TAs) 69–70
teaching talk 103
thinking aloud 50, 99, 101–102
Thomas, G. 59, 61, 62, 67
Thompson, R.A. 6
Thousand, J.S. 68
three mountains task 15
Timperley, H. 81
Tod, J. 88
Tomlinson, S. 61
Torgerson, C.J. 42

Torrance, H. 78
training 41, 45, 67–68
trauma 10, 18, 19, 87
Tregaskis, C. 63
Trundley, R. 69
Tunmer, W.E. 42

United Education 58

very able pupils 70
Vickerman, P. 59
Villa, R.A. 68
visual representations 6, 15–16, 28, 34, 39, 49, 51, 71
visualisers 51–52
visuospatial sketch pad 26–29
vocabulary 2, 3, 23, 43, 44
Vygotsky, L.S. 17, 49

Walton, P.D. 42
Watson, J. 41
Webb, M. 74, 78
Weisberg, D. 1
Wiliam, D. 74
Wilson, J. 60
Winch, C. 105
word recognition 42, 43–44
working memory 2, 10, 25, 26–29, 30–31
World Health Organization 66
writing/literacy 2, 3, 36, 41, 100, 102; *see also* phonics
Wyse, D. 42

Zimmerman, B.J. 99
zone of proximal development 17, 23, 49